Simply Chocolate

Irresistible recipes to share with friends and family

Janelle Bloom

VIKING

Viking
Penguin Books Australia Ltd
487 Maroondah Highway, PO Box 257
Ringwood, Victoria 3134, Australia
Penguin Books Ltd
Harmondsworth, Middlesex, England
Viking Penguin, A Division of Penguin Books USA Inc.
375 Hudson Street, New York, New York 10014, USA
Penguin Books Canada Limited
10 Alcorn Avenue, Toronto, Ontario, Canada M4V 3B2
Penguin Books (N.Z.) Ltd
Cnr Rosedale and Airborne Roads, Albany, Auckland, New Zealand

First published by Penguin Books Australia Ltd 1997

10 9 8 7 6 5 4 3 2 1

Copyright © Janelle Bloom, 1997

Design by Glenn Thomas, Penguin Design Studio
Food styling by Janelle Bloom
Cooking assistants Sharon Burge and Wendy Ryan
Photography by Barry Campbell
Photography on pages 24, 26, 76, 78, 130, 136 and 142 by Andre Martin
Typeset in 10/14 pt Giovanni by Midland Typesetters, Maryborough, Victoria
Produced by The Australian Book Connection

National Library of Australia
Cataloguing-in-Publication data

Bloom, Janelle.
    Simply chocolate : irresistible recipes to share
    with friends and family.

    ISBN 0 670 87844 8.

    1. Cookery (Chocolate). I. Title.

641.6374

Contents

Acknowledgments

There are many people who have contributed to this cookbook. Whether it was just a little or a lot, I wish to thank the following, as I would not have been able to get this book completed successfully without them.

The biggest thankyou goes to my family and close friends who have continued to support and keep in contact with me even though I have had no social time for anyone over the past 2 years. To my fabulous sisters, Sharon and Wendy (whom I adore), who tested all my recipes as 'non-professionals' and assisted me during the photography; Geoff Yates, who managed this project like the professional he is and put up with many late nights and weekend phone calls; Julie Ferguson, a very talented young home economist/food stylist from 'What's Cooking', who gave me a few of her favourite chocolate recipes to include in this book; Julie Gibbs and the fabulous team at Penguin Books for helping another one of my dreams become a reality; Lindy Vianellos, Tiffany Muller and Nestlé Confectionery Ltd, who supported this book when it was just a concept; Sharon, Deb and Karen at Lintas Sprint for believing in my ability to produce quality recipes; Barry Campbell, the photographer who worked with me (and against me at times) every step of the way to produce photographs that bring my food to life; Robin George, the secretary from heaven, who somehow was able to keep me focused on a deadline that seemed to sneak up on us; Antico's, for some of the very best fruit I have ever seen; Julie, Nat and the crew at NBN in Newcastle, who always work around my ever-changing schedules.

A special thankyou goes to the supervising producer, Peter Corrigan, at Channel 9's 'What's Cooking' for including me as part of the show for the past 5 years. To the rest of the team who started out as colleagues but quickly became good friends: everyone should be as lucky as I am to work with such a great bunch of people.

As you flick through this book it is impossible not to notice the stunning plates and accessories I have used. Many of these have been generously lent by Peter's of Kensington, NSW; Sirocco Homewares, Willoughby, NSW; Dinosaur Designs, Surry Hills, NSW; Country Floors, Willoughby, NSW; and Billygoat Boxes, Coogee, NSW. To them a heartfelt thanks.

Finally, I would like to thank some special friends: Robin, Glenda, Tracey, Cathy and Annette, who always seem to be there supporting me. I have been blessed with great friends.

Introduction

This book is about an obsession. It is not only my obsession, but one many people the world over share. Without a doubt the most universally irresistible dessert ingredient is chocolate, and as I am a confirmed 'chocoholic', writing a book about chocolate seemed the obvious choice for my second cookbook.

My first memories of chocolate go back to my childhood, when my grandparents used to visit. They always brought chocolate that was offered as a reward or bribe for us (my two sisters and me) to finish our vegetables. It became something of a family tradition, one many families still use!

As I grew older my love for cooking came from spending hours in the kitchen with my grandmother, who was the most amazing home cook. Some of her specialties were sliced-up crepes flooded with hot chocolate sauce, topped with meringue and then baked until the crepes were so tender they just melted in your mouth. Then there was my grandmother's chocolate kugelhopf – a yeast bun/cake that was filled with chocolate and baked. She would stand proudly over it as we lined up for a piece. Somehow I always got the slice that oozed lots of warm chocolate – an omen, I expect.

The first recipe I ever cooked was a chocolate mousse from *My Learn to Cook Book*. I remember waiting (it seemed like forever) with my sisters for the mousse to set. It never did, but we consumed and enjoyed it anyway, much to my mother's disgust. Years later, everyone I knew was getting a little bored with my latest favourite recipe, my aunt's chocolate fudge slice, so I was urged to progress. As a professional I did so, and have mastered many more chocolate delights that have become favourites with family and friends.

With so many chocolate cookbooks on the market I wondered if there was room for another. After much research I realised there was a need for reliable, foolproof recipes that were relatively quick and easy to prepare, and that used familiar, easy-to-find, affordable ingredients. I used this brief to compile all the recipes in this cookbook. My knowledge and experience with microwave ovens has allowed me to include microwave tips and instructions, where applicable, to help speed up the preparation time.

Those of my friends who openly admit to chocolate addiction all had a favourite recipe they wanted to contribute: chocolate recipes are usually connected to memorable occasions everyone wants to share. Chocolate is one of life's greatest pleasures, so I urge you to whip up a batch of Fudge Brownie Cookies, bake a Honeycomb Cheesecake, indulge in rich Chocolate Croissant Pudding. Just be sure you simply enjoy . . . *Simply Chocolate.*

A Few Helpful Tips

CREAM TIPS

My job has allowed me to travel and one of the many things I have noticed is that there are many types of cream available in different markets. As I have been specific about what cream I have used in the recipes in this cookbook, here is an insight into the different types available.

Clotted Cream   Also known as scalded cream, clotted cream has a fat content of 48%. It is available from gourmet food shops and some delicatessens. It is thick and rich and is usually served with scones and pikelets.

Creme Fraiche   Is a French term for fresh cream. It is a blend of pure cream and buttermilk or sour cream and has a fat content in excess of 40%. As it is unlikely to curdle when heated, creme fraiche is ideal for sauces, pasta dishes and fruity desserts. It is easy to make yourself. Combine 300 ml pure cream with 150 ml buttermilk or sour cream. Cover and allow the mixture to stand at room temperature for 6 hours. Refrigerate for 24 hours before using. Creme fraiche will keep for 10 days in the refrigerator.

Pouring Cream   (may sometimes be labelled Pure Cream) Is a thin pouring cream with a fat content of 35%. It is ideal for using as an ingredient in cakes, desserts, puddings and sauces. Pouring cream may be substituted for thickened cream.

Pure Cream   Also known as thick or double cream. It has a minimum fat content of 45%. Pure cream is ideal to serve on the side with cakes and desserts.

Reduced Cream   Has a fat content of 25% and is ideal in creamy sauces, drinks and cocktails. Reduced cream will *not* whip. See also 'Thickened cream'.

Thickened Cream   Is pouring cream that has had a small amount of gelatine or another stabilising agent added to produce a thicker cream. It has a fat content of 35%. The gelatine or stabiliser means that this cream is less likely to curdle or separate when whipped. Thickened cream can be substituted for pouring cream. Reduced-fat thickened cream contains 25% fat. Light thickened cream has a fat content of 18%. It is important to note that reduced-fat and light cream will *not* whip.

MICROWAVING TIPS

Microwave cooking is one of my specialties. I have worked with microwave ovens for over 15 years, so I have included a selection of microwave recipes in this cookbook. Some recipes have two sets of instructions – conventional and microwave – only when the microwave result is as good or better than the conventional result (see Self-saucing Peanut Bar Pudding on page 44). You will also find microwave tips throughout the entire book. These have been included where using the microwave reduces the time, makes the step easier or simply reduces the washing up. The microwave oven is a fabulous appliance when working with chocolate.

All microwave ovens are different, so the microwave instructions are written to cover the various brands on the market. For example on page 8, the microwave instructions read: Heat, uncovered, for 2 minutes on MEDIUM–HIGH/650 watts/70%. If you have a Sharp or a Panasonic microwave oven, always follow the HIGH, MEDIUM etc. instructions. If you own a Whirlpool microwave oven, follow the 800 watts/500 watts etc. instructions. (See the table below.)

Sharp	Panasonic	Whirlpool	Samsung	Sanyo
HIGH	800–850 watts	100%
MEDIUM–HIGH	650 watts	70%
MEDIUM	500 watts	50%
MEDIUM–LOW	350 watts	30%
DEFROST	160 watts	20%
LOW	90 watts	10%

BAKING TIPS

The recipes in this book have been tested using a fan-forced oven, which is 10–20°C hotter than a regular oven. Fan-forced ovens can dry out the surface of cakes, biscuits and slices. If you find this is the case, you may need to reduce the oven temperature and increase the cooking time. If you do not have a fan-forced oven, either increase the temperature by 10–20°C or cook the cake slightly longer. In both cases, check the cake regularly to ensure it does not overcook.

- All conventional ovens perform differently (some are hot, so temperatures need to be reduced; some cook slowly, so cooking times need to be extended). The recipes in this cookbook were tested in a fan-forced oven. Get to know how your oven performs and use my cooking times and recipes as a guide. As you become more confident, cook with common sense. A recipe is just an idea and should be changed to suit your likes and dislikes. This way my recipes will become yours, and they will get better and better.

- Line cake tins and baking trays with non-stick baking paper. I use Glad Bake.

- Always sift dry ingredients. This is important as it allows for aeration and the removal of any foreign particles. It will also help the ingredients blend thoroughly.

- When measuring ingredients, always be accurate. Use metric measuring cups and spoons and ensure measurements are level.

- When creaming butter and sugar, make sure the butter is at room temperature (not chilled or melted). If softening butter in the microwave oven, cut it into even-sized cubes and soften for 30 seconds at a time on MEDIUM–LOW/ 350 watts/30% power.

- Cakes are cooked when: the top of the cake springs back when pressed gently with the fingertips; the cake comes away from the side of the tin; a skewer inserted into the centre of the cake comes out clean and dry.

- If a freshly baked cake is too crumbly to ice, spread the cake with a very thin layer of softened butter. Place the cake in the freezer for 20 minutes, then ice.

- Position the rack in your oven just below the centre, so the cake is actually sitting in the centre of the oven while cooking.

- Make sure you always preheat the oven, otherwise cakes, slices and desserts will not get the lift they need. They will also take longer to cook and may dry out.

- Break eggs one at a time into a bowl before adding them to your ingredients – just in case an egg is not fresh.

- Lightly toast nuts and coconut in the oven or in a dry frying pan before adding them to your dishes. This releases the natural oils and brings out their flavour. As both nuts and coconut burn easily, keep an eye on them and give the tray or pan a shake occasionally while cooking.

- Allow a freshly baked cake to stand in its tin for 5–10 minutes before turning it out. This should prevent the cake from falling apart. Do not allow the cake to cool completely in the tin, unless the recipe specifies this, as it will cause the cake to sweat and it may stick.

- If using dried fruits, first soak them in alcohol or fruit juice. They will absorb the moisture and therefore help keep the cake moist.

- If adding orange, lemon or lime rind to cakes, biscuits or slices, always cream the rind with the butter and sugar to release its natural oils.

- For dense cakes, nuts can be roughly chopped; however, for lighter-textured cakes, grind nuts finely so they do not fall to the bottom of the cake.

- Avoid opening the oven door for at least the first three-quarters of the baking time. Then open it only sparingly to check on the progress. Opening the door too often may mean a fall in temperature that may in turn see your cake sink.

- Do not ice cakes, biscuits or slices until they are completely cooled, unless the recipe specifies that you do so.

- Wait until the cake is completely cool before placing it into an airtight container. The condensation from a warm cake will cause it to go soggy.

- If your cooking cake is brown enough on the top but not quite ready in the centre, cover it loosely with a sheet of greased aluminium foil.

- Use eggs at room temperature when baking. Adding cold eggs to creamed butter will cause the mixture to curdle. If eggs are from the refrigerator, place them (before use) in a bowl of warm water for a few minutes.

- To blind bake a pastry case, cover the pastry with aluminium foil and weigh it down with dried beans, rice or special baking weights. Bake for 15 minutes at the specified temperature, then remove the beans and foil and return the pastry case to the oven until golden. This process results in a crisp, even base (the beans stop the pastry from rising).

Throughout the recipes in this cookbook, the symbol ✎ refers to a helpful cooking tip. The symbol ▨ refers to a microwaving short cut.

The World's Favourite Flavour

The rewards of baking with chocolate are endless; however, the world's favourite flavour can be a little temperamental at times. This chapter is, therefore, very important. The information that follows is gathered from years of experience but will take only a few minutes to read. Then it's happy cooking with simply chocolate.

Understanding Chocolate

THE VARIETIES OF CHOCOLATE

The main ingredients of chocolate are cocoa liquor, cocoa butter and sugar. The texture and flavour of chocolate are governed by the varying properties of these key ingredients.

DARK CHOCOLATE/COOKING CHOCOLATE

Contains varying amounts of sugar, cocoa liquor, cocoa butter and vanilla. It has a strong, rich flavour and is the type of chocolate I prefer to use when making that unforgettable mousse or chocolate cake. This chocolate, however, needs more attention in the preparation for melting and must be tempered when used for coating, piping or moulding (however it does not need to be tempered for general baking uses). I explain tempering on page 5. During the preparation of this cookbook, I used Plaistowe Cooking Chocolate because it is Australian, it is widely available, it is in pristine quality when purchased, it is reasonably priced and it delivers that strong, rich chocolate flavour my friends never forget!

MILK CHOCOLATE

Contains the same ingredients as dark chocolate with milk solids being added during the manufacturing process. It is lighter in colour and is not as rich in flavour as dark chocolate.

WHITE CHOCOLATE

There is some discrepancy about whether white chocolate should be classified as 'real' chocolate. Essentially, it contains cocoa butter, sugar and milk solids but has no cocoa liquor. It is rich and creamy and is noticeably sweeter than dark and milk chocolate.

COUVERTURE CHOCOLATE

'Couverture' is French for coating, which is to what this high-quality product is particularly suited. It contains the highest percentage of cocoa butter and cocoa liquor of any of the chocolate products, which makes it very smooth and rich. Couverture chocolate needs to be tempered (see page 5) when used for coating, dipping or piping. It is available at specialty shops and is much more expensive than dark chocolate, but it delivers the very best chocolate flavour of all.

CHOC BITS

Are available in dark, milk and white chocolate. They are pure chocolate pieces containing cocoa butter. They have a high fat content, which means they will retain their shape when baked in biscuits, muffins and slices. They are easy to measure and can be melted and used as pure chocolate, but best of all, any leftovers from cooking can be consumed and enjoyed.

COMPOUND CHOCOLATE/CHOC MELTS

The purists will shudder to see 'compound' and 'chocolate' mentioned in the same sentence. Compound chocolate contains similar ingredients to cooking and eating chocolate, however the cocoa butter has been removed and replaced by vegetable fats/oil. The inclusion of vegetable fats means compound chocolate is less expensive, easier to melt/handle, quicker to set (it will set at room temperature) and does not need to be tempered for dipping, moulding or piping. Compound chocolate does not have the intense flavour or smooth mouth feel of 'real' chocolate, however it is foolproof, reliable, less expensive and widely available. Compound chocolate is ideal for kids' cakes, muffins, icing, moulding and dipping.

COCOA

Is a dry, fine, highly concentrated powder with a bitter taste. During the manufacturing process, most of the cocoa butter is removed from the cocoa liquor, leaving unsweetened cocoa. Cocoa is relatively low in fat compared to chocolate. It delivers an intense, rich flavour to cakes, desserts and drinks. I use Nestlé Baking Cocoa as it is pure and does not contain any sweetening agents.

STORING CHOCOLATE

There are many varied opinions about how chocolate should be stored. The following information has been compiled from my own experiences.

Unopened chocolate should be stored in a cool, dry place. A pantry or storage cupboard is ideal. Opened chocolate should be wrapped in aluminium foil and stored in an airtight container in a cool, dry place.

Sometimes chocolate will 'bloom'. This usually occurs when the chocolate has been stored at temperatures higher than 25°C; the cocoa butter begins to melt and the surface of the chocolate becomes grey. It doesn't affect the flavour but it is unappetising to serve. The 'bloom' is not a sign of freshness: the only way to check the freshness of chocolate is to taste it. Stale chocolate has a dry, crumbly texture, is unpleasant to taste and may also have 'bloomed'.

My advice on the subject of storing chocolate is to purchase enough chocolate for your short-term needs (with a little extra for those cravings). However, if you have an excess of chocolate for your immediate needs, wrap it well in foil and freeze it for up to 6 months. Allow the chocolate to come to room temperature while it is still wrapped in the foil before using it.

MELTING CHOCOLATE

Melting chocolate is not as simple as putting the chocolate into a saucepan or bowl, placing it on the stove or in the microwave and walking away. **Always** be close by when you are melting chocolate. Chocolate scorches easily and, once scorched, you will have to discard it and start again.

CONVENTIONAL METHODS

Over simmering water   Place the chocolate in a heat-resistant bowl or in the top of a double boiler over a saucepan of simmering water. The base of the bowl or pan containing the chocolate must not come into contact with the water because the excessive heat will cause the chocolate to burn. No steam should escape from around the sides of the bowl, as the steam will form condensation on the surface of the melting chocolate and will cause the chocolate to seize. Place the base saucepan over a low heat and allow the chocolate to melt slowly, stirring often.

In the oven   Preheat the oven to 160°C (315°F) for 15 minutes. Turn off the oven. Chop or break the chocolate into small pieces. Place the chocolate in a heat-resistant bowl and transfer the bowl to the oven. Check the chocolate frequently to be sure it is not burning, especially the edges in contact with the bowl.

Over direct heat   This is not a method I recommend. However, if there is no other choice or you are melting the chocolate with other ingredients such as cream or butter, it should be done in a small, heavy-based saucepan over a very low heat, stirring constantly. As soon as the chocolate has melted remove the saucepan from the heat and transfer the chocolate to another bowl.

MICROWAVING

Microwaving is a great way to melt pure and compound chocolate, however the procedure for both types of chocolate is not the same. I prefer to melt pure chocolate or couverture on MEDIUM/500 watts/50% and compound chocolate on MEDIUM–HIGH/650 watts/70%.

   Break or chop the chocolate into even pieces. Place the chocolate in a clean, dry heat-resistant bowl. Heat, uncovered, in 1-minute bursts (on MEDIUM for pure chocolate and MEDIUM–HIGH for compound chocolate). Stir the chocolate until smooth and transfer it to a clean bowl. Repeat the process until the chocolate has been melted. Here are a few extra microwaving tips:

- Use a clean, dry heat-resistant bowl, not plastic. Plastic dishes can retain moisture that will cause the chocolate to seize (to clump and become grainy).

- Chocolate will hold its shape when melting in the microwave oven, so it is very important to stir after each minute.

- Always melt chocolate uncovered. If it is covered, condensation will build up and may drop moisture into the chocolate, which will cause it to seize.

- Take melted chocolate from the microwave oven when slightly underdone, and let stand for 30 seconds. The internal heat and the heat from the bowl will continue to melt the chocolate.

TEMPERING CHOCOLATE

Pure chocolate and couverture chocolate are high in cocoa butter and cocoa liquor and need to go through a tempering process when used for moulding chocolates or making confectionery. The tempering process ensures the chocolate will set, giving a shiny, 'professional' finish.

Break the chocolate into even pieces and place in the top of a double saucepan or a heatproof bowl. Place the saucepan or bowl over a saucepan of simmering water, making sure that the water does not touch the base of the pan or bowl. Gently stir the chocolate until it has melted and it reaches 45°C. Use a candy thermometer to measure the temperature, being careful not to rest it on the bottom of the bowl or pan. Remove the pan/bowl from the heat and sit in a bowl of cold water. Stir constantly until the chocolate thickens and begins to set around the edges – the chocolate should reach 27°C. Return the pan/bowl to the pan of simmering water and stir constantly until the chocolate melts again and reaches 32°C. The chocolate is now tempered. To test: place a small dollop of chocolate onto non-stick baking paper and allow to stand at room temperature. The chocolate should set to a high gloss within a few minutes.

CHOCOLATE DECORATING IDEAS

Chocolate Bubbles   Melt 100 g dark, milk or white melts. Take a clean, unused sheet of bubble wrap and spread the chocolate over the textured surface. Allow the chocolate to set at room temperature. Carefully peel the bubble wrap away from the chocolate, then break the chocolate into the desired sizes. (See page 109.)

Chocolate Circles   Draw the desired size circles onto sheets of non-stick baking paper and place on baking trays. Melt 100 g dark, milk or white melts, then using a paper piping bag or the corner of a storage bag and following the outlines drawn, pipe circles in a continuous motion. Allow the chocolate to set before using a palette knife to lift the circles from the paper and transfer them to your dessert. (See page 139.)

Chocolate Curls   Melt 100 g dark, milk or white melts. Spread a thin layer onto a flat surface (such as a marble slab, back of a baking tray or chopping board). Allow the chocolate to set at room temperature. Using a sharp, long-bladed knife at a 45° angle to the chocolate, scrape strips of chocolate away from you. If the curls are breaking, it is because the chocolate has set too firmly and needs to be re-melted. Curls are great decorations (see page 19), but they take a little patience and practice.

Chocolate Drizzles   Melt 150 g dark, milk or white melts, then using a paper piping bag or the corner of a storage bag, drizzle or swirl the chocolate onto a baking tray lined with non-stick baking paper. Allow the chocolate to set before carefully lifting it off with a palette knife.

   To obtain half-moon-style drizzles (as seen on page 51), wrap a sheet of non-stick baking paper around a rolling pin or the cardboard roll from aluminium foil or plastic wrap. Secure the ends with tape or a paper clip. Pipe thin drizzles of chocolate backwards and forwards over the roll. Allow the chocolate to set before carefully peeling the paper away from it.

Chocolate Leaves   Using a clean, dry brush, brush the underside of non-toxic leaves, such as camellia, ivy and rose leaves, with melted dark, milk or white melts. If you can see the leaf through the chocolate, apply a second coat. Allow the chocolate to set. Always peel the leaf away from the chocolate, not the chocolate away from the leaf.

Chocolate Shapes   Melt 150 g dark, milk or white melts. Line a flat surface (baking tray or chopping board) with a sheet of non-stick baking paper. Spread the chocolate to an even thickness and allow it to set at room temperature. Using a biscuit cutter, carefully cut out shapes. Place the shapes onto a second piece of baking paper and refrigerate them until firm before using them to decorate cakes, desserts or slices. If the chocolate has set too firmly, the shapes will crack as you ease the cutter into the chocolate. If this happens, hold a hair dryer on low over the surface to soften the chocolate.

Chocolate Shavings   Use a clean, dry vegetable peeler to grate a block of chocolate. Place a sheet of non-stick baking paper onto the work surface and grate the chocolate directly over the paper. Grated or shaved chocolate (as seen on page 35) is ideal for the top of drinks, cakes and desserts.

Chocolate Squares or Triangles   Cover a 20-cm square board with a sheet of non-stick baking paper. Alternatively, line a 20-cm square cake tin. Spread 200 g melted dark, milk or white melts over the paper. Allow the chocolate to set at room temperature. Using a ruler and a sharp knife, cut the chocolate into squares, and the squares into triangles, if desired. Place the chocolate shapes in the refrigerator until firm enough to use as decoration.

Chocolate Sticks   Melt 100 g dark, milk or white melts. Using a paper piping bag or the corner of a storage bag, pipe thin lines onto a baking tray lined with non-stick baking paper. Allow the chocolate to set, then break it into the desired lengths (as seen on page 63).

Quick and Easy

The combination of today's busy lifestyles and the many cake shops that have popped up means that we have less time and less need to bake those memorable treats many of us enjoyed while growing up. I hope the recipes in this chapter encourage you to cook a little more and pass on that home-cooked experience to your family and friends. These recipes are easy to prepare and cook – in less than an hour – and are even easier to consume. They feature affordable and easy-to-obtain ingredients. This chapter also features my favourite recipe in this book: Peanut-butter-lovers' Cookies. They are quick, easy, and just melt in the mouth, with their wonderful cooking aroma lasting for hours!

Cappuccino Mousse

The combination of coffee and chocolate is sublime. This recipe came from a brainstorming session with a special friend.

SERVES: 6
PREPARATION TIME:
15 minutes, plus chilling time
COOKING TIME:
2–3 minutes
CHILLING TIME:
2–3 hours

MOUSSE
200 g cooking chocolate
1 tablespoon coffee powder
¼ cup hot water
3 egg yolks
2 egg whites
2 tablespoons caster sugar
150 ml thickened cream

TOPPING
150 ml thickened cream
1 egg white
2 tablespoons caster sugar
cocoa, for dusting

biscuits or almond bread, to serve

Do not beat the cream past the soft peak stage, as it will become too thick to fold into the mousse.

Place the chocolate, coffee and water in a large heatproof bowl. Heat, uncovered, for 2 minutes on MEDIUM–HIGH/650 watts/70%. Remove the mixture and stir until well combined.

1 MOUSSE Place the chocolate, coffee and water in a small saucepan over a low heat and stir, uncovered, until the chocolate has melted. (Alternatively, see the microwave tip.) Remove the pan from the heat and transfer the chocolate mixture to a large bowl. Add the egg yolks and mix well.

2 Using an electric mixer, beat the egg whites until soft peaks form. Gradually add the sugar and beat until the mixture is thick and glossy and the sugar has dissolved. Fold the egg white and sugar mixture into the chocolate mixture. Beat the cream until soft peaks form, and fold this into the chocolate mixture.

3 Spoon the chocolate mixture into a large serving bowl or 6 individual glasses. Cover with plastic wrap and refrigerate for 2–3 hours, or until firm.

4 TOPPING Just before serving, beat the cream and the egg white in separate bowls until soft peaks form. Gradually add the sugar to the egg white and beat until the mixture is thick and glossy and the sugar has dissolved. Fold the egg white mixture into the cream and spoon on top of the mousse. Dust with the cocoa.

5 Serve immediately with biscuits or almond bread.

Peanut-butter-lovers' Cookies

For those of you who love peanut butter, this recipe will quickly become a favourite – as it has with many of my friends.

MAKES:
approximately 30
PREPARATION TIME:
10 minutes
COOKING TIME:
20 minutes

Do not overcook the cookies; they will crisp on cooling.

375 g smooth peanut butter
1 egg
1 cup caster sugar
¹/₂ **cup Nestlé Milk Choc Bits**

¹/₂ **cup Nestlé White Choc Bits**

100 g milk chocolate melts, melted (optional)

1 Preheat the oven to 180°C (350°F). Grease 2 baking trays and line with non-stick baking paper.

2 In a large bowl, combine the peanut butter, egg and sugar, mixing well. Then add the milk Choc Bits and the white Choc Bits, mixing well.

3 Roll 1 tablespoon of the mixture into a ball. Repeat until all the mixture is used. Place the balls onto the prepared trays, allowing room for spreading, and flatten them slightly. Place the trays in the oven and bake for 12–15 minutes, or until the biscuits are a light golden colour. Allow the cookies to cool slightly on the trays before transferring to a wire rack.

4 When the cookies are cold, drizzle the tops with milk melts, if desired.

Citrus Cocoa Biscuits

MAKES: *24*
PREPARATION TIME:
10 minutes
COOKING TIME:
12 minutes

1 cup self-raising flour
¼ cup cocoa
1 cup caster sugar
1 egg yolk
125 g butter, melted

grated rind of 1 orange, 1 lemon
   and 1 lime
1 tablespoon fresh orange juice
1 cup desiccated coconut
60 g milk chocolate melts, melted

When baking 2 trays of biscuits at a time, position one rack just below the centre of your oven and one rack just above. Check the biscuits after 8–10 minutes: the trays may need to be switched around, depending on how evenly your oven distributes heat.

1. Preheat the oven to 180°C (350°F). Grease 2 baking trays and line with non-stick baking paper.

2. Sift the flour and cocoa into a large bowl. Add the sugar and stir until well combined.

3. Combine the egg yolk, butter, citrus rind and orange juice in a small bowl. Add the egg mixture to the dry ingredients, then mix well. Roll 1 tablespoon of the mixture into a ball and then roll it in the coconut. Repeat until all the mixture has been used.

4. Place the balls onto the prepared baking trays and flatten slightly, allowing plenty of room for spreading. Bake for 12 minutes. Allow the biscuits to cool slightly on the trays before transferring to a wire rack to cool completely.

5. When the biscuits are cold, drizzle the tops with the milk melts and allow the chocolate to set before serving.

Microwave Fudge Brownies

I decided to include this recipe from my Microwave Cookbook *because it became a real favourite with many TV and radio announcers when I was on the publicity tour.*

MAKES: *16*

PREPARATION TIME:
10 minutes

COOKING TIME:
16 minutes

Roasting racks are an essential microwave accessory. They are ideal for defrosting, reheating, and cooking cakes and delicate foods. They elevate dishes off the turntable, which helps to ensure even microwave cooking/ heating.

125 g butter
1½ cups brown sugar
2 teaspoons vanilla essence
3 eggs
200 g cooking chocolate
¾ cup plain flour, sifted
150 g walnuts, chopped

TOPPING

½ cup Nestlé White Choc Bits
½ cup Nestlé Milk Choc Bits
100 g walnuts

ice-cream, cream or Chocolate Sauce (see page 65), to serve

1. Grease a 20-cm square microwave-safe and heatproof glass dish and line with non-stick baking paper.

2. Cream the butter and brown sugar until pale in colour. Add the vanilla essence and eggs, mixing well. (Do not be concerned if the mixture curdles.)

3. Place the chocolate in a clean, dry heatproof bowl, and heat, uncovered, in the microwave for 2–3 minutes on MEDIUM/500 watts/50%, or until melted. Stir the melted chocolate into the butter mixture.

4. Fold in the flour and walnuts. Spread the mixture into the prepared dish. Place on a microwave-safe roasting rack and cook in the microwave, uncovered, for 10 minutes on MEDIUM/500 watts/50%.

5. *TOPPING* Carefully scatter the topping ingredients over the half-cooked brownie. Cook, uncovered, for a further 5–6 minutes on MEDIUM/500 watts/ 50%. Refrigerate the brownie overnight.

6. Serve the brownie cut into slices with ice-cream, cream or Chocolate Sauce, if you want to be totally decadent.

Plum Cake

I have fond memories of my mother baking plum cakes when I was young. We eagerly awaited her turning out the cake, and we'd devour it while still hot.

SERVES: 8
PREPARATION TIME:
15 minutes
COOKING TIME:
approximately
1 hour

When plums are not in season or as an alternative, try making this cake with peaches, nectarines or 200 g blueberries.

6–8 plums
150 g butter
³⁄₄ cup caster sugar
1 teaspoon vanilla essence
3 eggs
100 g milk chocolate melts, melted
2 cups self-raising flour
¹⁄₄ cup milk

TOPPING

¹⁄₄ cup slivered almonds
¹⁄₂ teaspoon cinnamon
1 teaspoon caster sugar

1. Preheat the oven to 160°C (315°F). Grease a 20-cm round cake tin and line with non-stick baking paper.

2. Cut the plums in half and remove the stones, then cut the plum halves in half.

3. Cream the butter, sugar and vanilla essence until light and fluffy. Add the eggs one at a time, mixing well after each addition (do not be concerned if the mixture curdles). Fold in the milk melts, sifted flour and milk. Spoon half the mixture into the prepared tin, top with half the plums, then spread over the remaining cake mixture. Press the remaining plum quarters into the top.

4. *TOPPING*   Combine the almonds, cinnamon and caster sugar and sprinkle over the cake batter.

5. Bake the cake for 1 hour–1 hour 20 minutes or until cooked when tested with a skewer. (Insert a skewer in the centre of the cake; if it comes out clean, the cake is cooked.) After 1 hour, cover the cake loosely with foil to prevent it browning too much. Allow the cake to cool in the tin for 20 minutes before turning it out. Serve warm.

Chocolate Caramel Tartlets

Caramel and chocolate is a match made in heaven and these tartlets are divine.

MAKES: *24*
PREPARATION TIME:
10 minutes
COOKING TIME:
30 minutes

24 frozen sweet shortcrust tartlet cases
60 g cooking chocolate, melted

FILLING
60 g butter
3 tablespoons golden syrup
400 g sweetened condensed milk

CHOCOLATE GANACHE
125 g cooking chocolate
125 g butter

chocolate curls (see page 5) (optional)

Place the butter, golden syrup and sweetened condensed milk in a heatproof bowl. Cook, uncovered, stirring every minute, for 3–4 minutes on HIGH/800 watts/ 100% or until the mixture resembles caramel.

Place the chocolate and butter in a heatproof bowl. Cook, uncovered, for 3–5 minutes on MEDIUM/500 watts/ 50%, stirring every minute until melted and well combined.

1 Preheat the oven to 180°C (350°F).

2 Place the frozen tartlet cases (leaving the pastry in the foil cases) onto a baking tray, then cook for 12–15 minutes, or until a light golden colour. Remove from the oven. Allow the tartlet cases to cool slightly, then brush the base of each tartlet case with the chocolate. Allow the chocolate to set.

3 *FILLING* In a medium saucepan, combine the butter, golden syrup and sweetened condensed milk. Cook over a medium heat, stirring constantly, for 5–6 minutes, or until the mixture resembles caramel. (Alternatively, see the first microwave tip.) Set aside to cool.

4 Spoon the caramel mixture into the tartlet cases. Place them in the oven and bake for 8–10 minutes at 180°C (350°F), or until the edges start to caramelise. Allow the tartlets to cool.

5 *CHOCOLATE GANACHE* Place the chocolate and butter in a small saucepan. Stir constantly over a low heat until they are melted and well combined. (Alternatively, see the second microwave tip.) Remove from the heat and transfer to a bowl. Allow to cool at room temperature until the mixture is thick enough for piping.

6 Decorate the tartlets with the Chocolate Ganache and chocolate curls, if desired, and serve immediately.

Raspberry Coconut Tartlets

This recipe was inspired by a popular American treat called Amy Johnson Cake. Even if you're not a big fan of currants, I guarantee you will enjoy them in these tarts.

MAKES: *12*

PREPARATION TIME:
20 minutes

COOKING TIME:
25 minutes

12 frozen sweet shortcrust tartlet cases
100 g white chocolate melts
⅓ cup raspberry jam
¾ cup currants

⅓ cup water
⅓ cup caster sugar
30 g butter
1¼ cups desiccated coconut
¼ teaspoon baking powder
1 egg

Place the water and sugar in a medium heatproof bowl. Cook, uncovered, stirring every minute, for 2–3 minutes on HIGH/ 850 watts/100%, or until the sugar has dissolved. Cook without stirring for a further 2 minutes on HIGH/800 watts/ 100%.

1   Preheat the oven to 180°C (350°F).

2   Place the frozen tartlet cases (leaving the pastry in the foil cases) onto a baking tray and cook for 8–10 minutes, or until light golden in colour. Remove from the oven and allow the tartlet cases to cool slightly.

3   Melt half the white melts in a heatproof bowl for 1–2 minutes on HIGH/800 watts/100% in the microwave. Spread evenly over the base of each tartlet case.

4   Combine the raspberry jam and currants. Spoon the mixture evenly into the tartlet cases.

5   Meanwhile, place the water and sugar in a medium saucepan over a medium heat and stir until the sugar has dissolved. Simmer for 3 minutes without stirring. Remove the pan from the heat and allow the mixture to cool slightly. (Alternatively, see the microwave tip.)

6   Finely chop the remaining white melts. Add the butter, coconut, baking powder, egg and chopped white melts to the sugar syrup and mix well. Spoon the coconut mixture evenly over the currant mixture.

7   Place the filled tartlet cases in the oven and cook at 180°C (350°F) for 15 minutes or until golden. Serve cold.

Robbie's Chocolate Caramel Slice

This recipe belongs to a very special friend who has contributed in many ways to this book.

MAKES: 35

PREPARATION TIME:
20 minutes

COOKING TIME:
50 minutes

For easy cutting, allow the slice to stand at room temperature for 30 minutes first.

Place the copha in a heatproof bowl. Heat, uncovered, stirring every minute, for 4 minutes on MEDIUM–HIGH/650 watts/70%. Add the chocolate and stir until it has melted – the heat from the copha will melt the chocolate.

BASE

1 cup plain flour
½ cup brown sugar
½ cup desiccated coconut
125 g butter, melted

FILLING

400 g sweetened condensed milk
2 tablespoons golden syrup
3 tablespoons butter, melted

TOPPING

125 g cooking chocolate
60 g copha, roughly chopped

1 Preheat the oven to 180°C (350°F). Grease a 28 × 18-cm lamington tin and line with non-stick baking paper.

2 BASE   Sift the flour into a mixing bowl. Mix in the brown sugar and coconut. Pour the melted butter over the dry ingredients and mix well. Press the base into the prepared tin.

3 Bake in the oven for 15–20 minutes, or until the base is a light golden colour. Remove the base from the oven and allow to cool slightly.

4 FILLING   Mix the sweetened condensed milk, golden syrup and melted butter. Pour the caramel over the cooked base. Place the filled base in the oven at 180°C (350°F) and cook for 20 minutes, or until the caramel is firm. Remove the slice from the oven and allow it to cool. Refrigerate for 3–4 hours or overnight, if possible.

5 TOPPING   Place the chocolate and copha in the top of a double boiler or in a bowl over simmering water. Make sure that the water does not touch the base of the bowl. Stir until the chocolate and copha are melted and well combined. (Alternatively, see the microwave tip.) Carefully pour the topping over the caramel and refrigerate until set. Cut into squares or triangles to serve.

Apricot and Pear Crumble Slice

All the recipes in this book are delicious – this one is also good for you.

MAKES: *16*

PREPARATION TIME:
20 minutes

COOKING TIME:
25 minutes

*Place all the filling
ingredients in a
medium bowl. Cook,
uncovered, for 7–10
minutes on HIGH/
800 watts/100% or
until the fruit has
softened and
absorbed the liquid.*

*Combine the
coconut and oats in
an oven bag. Twist
the bag to secure
and cook, shaking
the bag gently every
minute, for 2–3
minutes on HIGH/
800 watts/100%.
Heat the butter and
golden syrup in a
medium bowl for
1 minute on HIGH/
800 watts/100%.
Stir in the toasted
coconut mixture.*

BASE
100 g dark chocolate melts
125 g butter
½ cup brown sugar
1 teaspoon vanilla essence
1 cup desiccated coconut
¾ cup plain flour, sifted
¼ cup cocoa, sifted

FILLING
250 g dried apricots, roughly
    chopped
250 g dried pears, roughly
    chopped

¾ cup water
grated rind of 1 orange
⅓ cup orange juice

TOPPING
¾ cup desiccated coconut
¾ cup rolled oats
60 g butter
2 tablespoons golden syrup

1   *BASE*   Preheat the oven to 180°C (350°F). Grease a 20-cm square cake tin and line with non-stick baking paper.

2   Place the dark melts and butter in a medium saucepan then stir over a medium heat until the butter and chocolate have melted. Remove from heat. Stir in the brown sugar, vanilla essence, coconut, flour and cocoa. Press the base mixture into the prepared tin.

3   Bake the base in the oven for 10 minutes. Remove the base from the oven and allow it to cool. It will firm on standing.

4   *FILLING*   Meanwhile, place all the filling ingredients in a saucepan and cook over a medium heat, stirring constantly, until the apricots have softened and absorbed the liquid. (Alternatively, see the first microwave tip.) Allow the filling to cool, then spread it over the cooled base.

5   *TOPPING*   Combine the coconut and oats in a dry frying pan. Cook over a medium heat, stirring constantly, until they are toasted. Melt the butter and golden syrup in a saucepan, then add the coconut and oats and stir until the mixture is well combined. (Alternatively, see the second microwave tip.) Spread the crumble mixture over the fruit filling.

6   Bake the assembled slice in the oven and cook at 180°C (350°F) for 15–20 minutes, or until cooked when tested with a skewer. (Insert a skewer in the centre of the slice; if it comes out clean, the slice is cooked.) Allow the slice to cool before cutting into squares.

Jelly Slice

This recipe is not just for the kids: it should be enjoyed by the whole family.

MAKES: 24
PREPARATION TIME:
*30 minutes, plus
chilling and setting
time*
COOKING TIME:
10 minutes
CHILLING TIME:
*approximately
2 hours*
SETTING TIME:
*approximately
3 hours*

BASE

125 g Marie biscuits, crushed
100 g butter, melted
125 g milk chocolate melts, melted

FILLING

1 tablespoon gelatine
2 tablespoons cold water
250 g cream cheese
400 g sweetened condensed milk
juice of 1 lemon
150 g white chocolate melts,
    melted

JELLY TOPPING

85 g raspberry, lime or lemon jelly
    crystals
1 cup boiling water

*1 tablespoon
gelatine =
1 × 10-g sachet.*

*Combine the
gelatine and water
in a small heatproof
bowl or jug. Heat,
uncovered, in the
microwave for 20
seconds on HIGH/
800 watts/100%,
stirring halfway
through heating.*

1　Grease a 28 × 18-cm lamington tin and line with non-stick baking paper.

2　*BASE*　Combine the biscuit crumbs, butter and milk melts in a large bowl. Mix the base ingredients until well combined, then press into the prepared tin. Refrigerate the base until it has set, 10–15 minutes.

3　*FILLING*　Combine the gelatine and water in a small saucepan and cook over a medium heat, stirring constantly, until the gelatine has dissolved. Allow the mixture to cool slightly. (Alternatively, see the microwave tip.)

4　Using an electric mixer, beat the cream cheese and sweetened condensed milk until well combined. Add the lemon juice and white melts, mixing well. Stir in the cooled gelatine mixture. Spread the filling over the base and refrigerate until set, 1–2 hours.

5　*JELLY TOPPING*　Meanwhile, ignoring the instructions on the packet, combine the jelly crystals with the boiling water in a heatproof jug. Allow the jelly to cool at room temperature. Pour the cooled jelly over the firm cream cheese filling and allow it to set in the refrigerator for 2–3 hours. (You may find it is easier to pour the jelly topping over the cream cheese while the slice is sitting flat in the refrigerator.) Using a warm knife, cut the slice into squares and serve.

Jules's Decadent Hazelnut Slice

This fabulous recipe was especially written for this book by a very talented friend, Julie from 'What's Cooking'. We hope you enjoy it.

MAKES: *20*

PREPARATION TIME: *10 minutes*

COOKING TIME: *10 minutes*

When lining the cake tin, ensure that you allow enough non-stick baking paper to come up the sides of the dish, so that when it comes to serving, the whole slice can be lifted out for easier slicing.

Place the hazelnut spread, dark melts, cream and butter in a medium heatproof bowl. Heat, uncovered, for 2 minutes on MEDIUM–HIGH/650 watts/70%. Stir until smooth.

BASE

250 g Marie biscuits, crushed
$1/2$ cup chocolate hazelnut spread
$1/2$ cup dark chocolate melts
$1/4$ cup pouring or thickened cream
60 g butter

TOPPING

$1/2$ cup chocolate hazelnut spread
$1/2$ cup pouring or thickened cream
100 g hazelnuts, toasted and roughly chopped

1 Grease a 20 × 26-cm rectangular cake tin and line with non-stick baking paper.

2 *BASE*   Place the crushed biscuits in a large mixing bowl.

3 Place the hazelnut spread, dark melts, cream and butter in a small saucepan. Cook over a low heat, stirring constantly, until the mixture is smooth. (Alternatively, see the microwave tip.) Add the hazelnut mixture to the biscuits and mix well.

4 Press the hazelnut and biscuit mixture over the base of the prepared tin.

5 *TOPPING*   Cook the hazelnut spread and cream in a small saucepan over a low heat, stirring constantly until the mixture is smooth. Pour the topping over the base. Tilt the tin to ensure the layer is even.

6 Sprinkle the top of the slice with the hazelnuts and refrigerate for 1 hour, or until the slice is well chilled.

7 Cut the slice into fingers with a hot knife and serve.

Chocolate Swirl Cheesecake Slice

This recipe was given to me by my sister Sharon. I'm sure she never expected to see it printed in a cookbook. Thanks, Sis!

MAKES: *12*
PREPARATION TIME: *20 minutes*
COOKING TIME: *40 minutes*

185 g butter
¼ cup cocoa
1 cup caster sugar
2 eggs
1 cup plain flour

250 g cream cheese, softened
⅓ cup caster sugar, extra
1 teaspoon vanilla essence
1 egg, extra

Try adding 1–2 tablespoons of Tia Maria or Kahlua to the chocolate mix. What a difference the alcohol can make!

Combine the butter and cocoa in a large heatproof bowl. Heat, uncovered, for 3–4 minutes on MEDIUM–HIGH/650 watts/70%. Mix the butter and cocoa until well combined.

1. Preheat the oven to 180°C (350°F). Grease a 28 × 18-cm lamington tin and line with non-stick baking paper.

2. Combine the butter and cocoa in a small saucepan over a medium heat and cook, stirring constantly, until the butter has melted and the cocoa has dissolved. (Alternatively, see the microwave tip.) Transfer the butter and cocoa to a large bowl. Add the 1 cup sugar, 2 eggs and flour, and mix well.

3. Pour the batter into the prepared tin and set aside.

4. Using an electric mixer, beat the cream cheese, extra sugar, and vanilla essence until light and fluffy. Add the extra egg and mix until well combined.

5. Carefully pour the cream cheese mixture over the chocolate mixture. Use a knife to swirl the two mixtures together in the tin. Place the slice in the oven and bake for about 40 minutes, or until a skewer inserted in the centre of the slice comes out clean. Allow the slice to cool in the tin before cutting into squares.

Super Chocolate Shake

MAKES: *2 tall glasses, plus 2 cups chocolate sauce*
PREPARATION TIME: *5 minutes, plus cooling time*
COOKING TIME: *5 minutes*

Store the remaining Chocolate Sauce in an airtight container or jar in the refrigerator. The sauce is great served warm over ice-cream, waffles or pancakes.

Place the dark melts and evaporated milk in a heatproof bowl or jug. Heat the chocolate and milk, stirring every minute, for 3–4 minutes on MEDIUM–HIGH/ 650 watts/70%.

2 cups icy cold milk
4 scoops of chocolate ice-cream

CHOCOLATE SAUCE
375 g dark chocolate melts
375 ml evaporated milk

1. CHOCOLATE SAUCE   Place the dark melts and evaporated milk in a medium saucepan, and cook over a medium heat, stirring constantly, until the sauce is smooth. (Alternatively, see the microwave tip.) Remove the sauce from the heat and pour into a clean jar. Allow the sauce to cool.

2. Place two large spoonfuls of Chocolate Sauce, the milk and 2 scoops of the ice-cream into a blender or milkshake maker and blend until the ingredients are well combined.

3. Pour the chocolate shake into 2 glasses, top each with a scoop of chocolate ice-cream and drizzle with extra chocolate sauce, if desired.

Rhonda's No-bake Slice

Rhonda is a very dear, chocoholic friend of my mother's. This is a recipe she says she attempts to file away but it always finds its way out again!

MAKES:
approximately 24
PREPARATION TIME:
10 minutes
SETTING TIME:
1½ hours

Combine the chocolate icing ingredients in a heatproof bowl with just enough hot water to make a thick paste. Heat, uncovered, for 30 seconds on HIGH/800 watts/ 100%.

125 g butter, melted
2 tablespoons cocoa
²/₃ cup brown sugar
1 egg, lightly beaten
250 g Nice biscuits, crushed

½ cup walnuts, finely chopped
½ cup sultanas
1 tablespoon sherry
Chocolate Icing 2 (see page 66)
100 g grated cooking chocolate

1 Grease a 25 × 18-cm cake tin and line with non-stick baking paper.

2 Combine the butter and cocoa in a large bowl and mix well, making sure the cocoa has dissolved.

3 Add the remaining base ingredients and mix until they are well combined. Press the mixture into the prepared tin, cover with plastic wrap and refrigerate for 1 hour, or until firm.

4 Spread the chocolate icing quickly over the slice. Sprinkle with the grated chocolate and allow the icing to set before cutting the slice into squares.

OPPOSITE: Rhonda's No-bake Slice (left) and Chewy Bubble Bars (see page 36).

►

Chewy Bubble Bars

This recipe is supposedly for the kids, but try keeping the adults away!

MAKES: *24*

PREPARATION TIME:
10 minutes

COOKING TIME:
5 minutes

SETTING TIME:
2 hours

Place the Chokito bars and butter in a large heatproof bowl. Heat, uncovered, for 3–4 minutes on MEDIUM–HIGH/650 *watts/70%. Stir until the mixture is well combined.*

4 × 60 g Nestlé Chokito, chopped
60 g butter

3 cups Rice Bubbles
¾ cup crushed nuts

1   Line a 28 × 18-cm lamington tin with non-stick baking paper.

2   Place the Chokito bars and the butter in a medium saucepan and cook over a medium heat, stirring constantly, until the Chokito bars have melted and the mixture has come together. (Alternatively, see the microwave tip.) Remove the pan from the heat and transfer the mixture to a large bowl.

3   Add the Rice Bubbles and nuts, and mix well.

4   Press the slice into the prepared tin. Refrigerate until the slice has set, approximately 2 hours. Cut into squares using a warm knife, and serve. (See photograph opposite page 34.)

Foolproof Favourites

Amongst the recipes most requested by family, friends and viewers of 'What's Cooking' are: brownies, mud cake, fudge cookies and muffins. So I thought that I would include all these indulgent recipes, and many more, in the one chapter, and test, retest and retest them again and again to make sure these favourites became a reliable collection of recipes for beginners and experts alike.

Roasted Hazelnut Brownies

I am a big fan of brownies – served as a slice or as a dessert. This mixture can also be cooked in a 23-cm round cake tin.

MAKES: *12*

PREPARATION TIME: *25 minutes*

COOKING TIME: *40 minutes*

125 g hazelnuts
200 g cooking chocolate
200 g butter
1½ cups brown sugar
4 eggs

½ cup plain flour
¼ cup self-raising flour
⅓ cup cocoa
extra cocoa and fresh fruit, to serve

Place the hazelnuts in an oven bag; twist to secure the bag. Place the bag in the microwave and cook for 3–5 minutes on HIGH/800 watts/ 100%, shaking the bag every minute.

Place the chocolate and butter in a large heatproof bowl. Cook, uncovered, stirring every minute, for 2–3 minutes on MEDIUM–HIGH/ 650 watts/70%.

1. Preheat the oven to 180°C (350°F).

2. Place the hazelnuts on a baking tray and roast in the oven for 15 minutes. (Alternatively, see the first microwave tip.) Remove the hazelnuts from the oven and allow them to cool. Place the nuts in a clean tea towel and rub them together to remove the skins. Reduce the oven temperature to 160°C (315°F). Roughly chop the nuts and put them to one side.

3. Grease a 28 × 18-cm lamington tin and line with non-stick baking paper.

4. Place the chocolate and butter in a small saucepan and cook over a medium heat, stirring constantly, until they have melted and are smooth. (Alternatively, see the second microwave tip.) Remove the chocolate mixture from the heat and transfer to a large bowl.

5. Add the brown sugar and eggs, and mix well.

6. Sift the flours and the cocoa and fold them into the chocolate mixture with the hazelnuts. Spread the brownie mixture into the prepared tin. Place in the oven and bake for 45–50 minutes or until the brownie is cooked (when a skewer inserted into the centre of the brownie mixture comes out clean). Allow the cake to cool in the tin before slicing.

7. Remove the brownies from the tin and dust with cocoa. Serve with fresh fruit.

Microwave Plum and Apple Crumble

Crumbles regularly appear on my dessert menu as they are quick and easy to make. The combination of chocolate and fruit in this crumble is sensational!

SERVES: 6–8

PREPARATION TIME: 15 minutes

COOKING TIME: 18 minutes

The combination for this recipe is only limited to your imagination. Try apple and raspberry; blueberries and pear; or mango, apple and passionfruit.

500 g blood plums
500 g Granny Smith apples
150 g butter
1½ cups wholemeal self-raising flour
²/₃ cup brown sugar

100 g NESTLÉ Milk Melts, roughly chopped
½ cup slivered almonds
custard, cream or ice-cream, to serve

1 Cut the plums in half and remove the stones, then cut the plum halves in half again. Peel, core and chop the apples.

2 Place the apples and plums in a 23-cm microwave-safe flan dish. Cover the dish with plastic wrap and cook for 6–8 minutes on HIGH/800 watts/100%, or until the fruit is just tender. Remove the plastic wrap carefully.

3 Rub the butter into the flour until the mixture resembles breadcrumbs. Stir in the brown sugar.

4 Sprinkle half the crumble over the fruit, top with the milk melts, then sprinkle on the remaining crumble. Sprinkle with the almonds. Cook the crumble for 5–6 minutes on MEDIUM–HIGH/650 watts/70%. Brown the crumble under a medium–hot grill, if desired.

5 Serve the crumble hot with custard, cream or ice-cream.

Buttermilk Hotcakes with Fruit and Butterscotch Sauce

I live by the beach, and Sunday brunches are a way of life. This recipe was inspired by a favourite dish often consumed at a local cafe in Newport, Sydney.

MAKES: 8
PREPARATION TIME:
10 minutes
COOKING TIME:
25 minutes

Place the butter, sugar, cream and white melts in a medium heatproof bowl. Heat, uncovered, whisking every minute, for 3–4 minutes on MEDIUM/500 watts/ 50% or until smooth. Add the fruit.

To warm the hotcakes, place them between sheets of damp paper towel and heat each for 30 seconds on MEDIUM/500 watts/ 50%.

HOTCAKES
1 cup self-raising flour
2 tablespoons caster sugar
½ teaspoon bicarbonate of soda
1 cup buttermilk
1 egg
1 teaspoon vanilla essence
50 g butter, melted
extra melted butter

BUTTERSCOTCH SAUCE
75 g butter
¼ cup brown sugar
½ cup pouring cream
100 g white chocolate melts
1 large banana, peeled and sliced
150 g fresh blueberries

1   *HOTCAKES*   Sift the flour, sugar and bicarbonate of soda into a large bowl. Add the buttermilk, egg, vanilla essence and 50 g melted butter. Stir until the mixture is combined.

2   Brush the base of a frying pan with the extra melted butter. Pour ¼ cup of the batter mixture into the frying pan, allowing room for the hotcake to spread. Cook the hotcake over a medium heat for 2–3 minutes, or until bubbles form on the surface. Carefully turn the hotcake over and cook for a further 1–2 minutes, or until the hotcake is cooked. Remove and keep warm. Continue until all the mixture has been used.

3   *BUTTERSCOTCH SAUCE*   Place the butter, brown sugar, cream and white melts in a medium saucepan. Cook the sauce over a medium heat, stirring constantly, until the chocolate has melted and the sauce is smooth. Add the banana slices and the blueberries. Cook for 1 minute, then remove from heat. (Alternatively, see the first microwave tip.)

4   Serve the hotcakes topped with fruit and the Butterscotch Sauce.

Self-saucing Peanut Bar Pudding

SERVES: 6–8
PREPARATION TIME:
15 minutes
COOKING TIME:
45 minutes

Self-saucing puddings can spill during cooking. To avoid a messy oven, place the pudding bowl onto a baking tray before placing into the oven.

2 cups self-raising flour, sifted
1 cup caster sugar
2 tablespoons NESTLÉ Baking Cocoa
100 g butter, melted
1 cup milk
2 × 40 g NESTLÉ SCORCHED PEANUT BAR, roughly chopped
1 cup brown sugar

2 tablespoons NESTLÉ Baking Cocoa, extra
2½ cups boiling water
icing sugar, for dusting

whipped cream or ice-cream, to serve (optional)
fresh fruit or berries, to serve (optional)

1 Preheat the oven to 180°C (350°F). Grease a 3-litre pudding bowl.

2 Sift the flour, sugar and cocoa into a large mixing bowl.

3 Combine the butter and milk, and add to the dry ingredients, mixing well. Fold the SCORCHED PEANUT BAR pieces through the chocolate batter, then spoon the mixture into the prepared pudding bowl.

4 Combine the brown sugar and extra cocoa, and sprinkle evenly over the pudding. Gently pour the boiling water over the pudding.

5 Place the pudding in the oven and bake for 45 minutes, or until the centre is firm to the touch. Allow to stand for 5 minutes before serving, dusted with icing sugar.

6 Serve with lashings of whipped cream or ice-cream and fresh fruit or berries, if desired.

MICROWAVE INSTRUCTIONS
- Lightly grease a 3-litre microwave-safe pudding bowl.
- Sift the flour, sugar and cocoa into a large mixing bowl.
- Combine the butter and milk, and add to the dry ingredients, mixing well. Fold the SCORCHED PEANUT BAR pieces through the chocolate batter, then spoon the mixture into the prepared pudding bowl.
- Combine the brown sugar and extra cocoa and sprinkle evenly over the pudding. Gently pour boiling water over the pudding.
- Cook the pudding, uncovered, for 20–25 minutes on MEDIUM–HIGH/650 watts/ 70%, or until the centre is just firm to the touch. Allow the pudding to stand for 10 minutes before dusting with the icing sugar.

Chocolate Croissant Pudding

This adaptation of the traditional bread-and-butter pudding has become a winter favourite amongst my friends.

SERVES: *6*

PREPARATION TIME: *10 minutes, plus 30 minutes standing time*

COOKING TIME: *35 minutes*

Stale croissants give the best results in this dish. Many bakeries sell day-old croissants at a reduced rate. These are ideal for this recipe.

Place the chocolate and cream in a medium heatproof bowl. Heat, uncovered, for 1–2 minutes on MEDIUM–HIGH/650 watts/70%, or until the chocolate has melted and the mixture is smooth.

100 g cooking chocolate
50 ml pouring or thickened cream
4 croissants
½ cup raisins

4 eggs
2 cups milk
1 teaspoon vanilla essence
2 tablespoons caster sugar

1. Grease a 6-cup baking dish or 6 × 1-cup pudding bowls.

2. Place the chocolate and cream into a medium saucepan and cook over a medium heat, stirring constantly, until the chocolate has melted and the mixture is smooth. (Alternatively, see the microwave tip.) Remove the chocolate cream from the heat and allow to cool and thicken.

3. Cut the croissants in half lengthwise. Spread them with the chocolate mixture and then close them up. Cut the croissants again – this time crosswise into four even pieces. Place the croissants in the prepared baking dish or pudding bowls. Evenly sprinkle the croissants with raisins.

4. Whisk together the eggs, milk, vanilla essence and caster sugar. Pour the custard over the croissants and allow the mixture to stand for 30 minutes.

5. Preheat the oven to 180°C (350°F). Place the pudding or puddings in the oven and bake for 25–30 minutes, or until a light golden colour and the custard has set. The centre may still be slightly soft, but this will firm on standing. Serve warm.

Heavenly Chocolate Custard

SERVES: 6
PREPARATION TIME:
20 minutes
COOKING TIME:
30 minutes

Heavenly Chocolate Custard is great served hot over Christmas pudding.

To reheat, place the custard in a heatproof jug in the microwave. Heat the custard, uncovered, stirring every minute, for 3–5 minutes on MEDIUM/500 watts/ 50%.

4 egg yolks
¼ cup caster sugar
1 teaspoon vanilla essence
2 tablespoons NESTLÉ Baking
    Cocoa
1 cup pouring cream

1 cup milk
100 g PLAISTOWE Cooking
    Chocolate, broken into squares

poached fruit, to serve (optional)

1 Cream the egg yolks, sugar and vanilla essence with a whisk until light and fluffy. Add the cocoa and whisk well.

2 In a medium saucepan bring the cream and milk to the boil. Remove the cream mixture from the heat and slowly pour it into the egg mixture, whisking continuously. Return the mixture to the saucepan and stir constantly over a low heat until the custard thickens slightly or coats the back of a metal spoon. Remove the custard from the heat, add the chocolate and stir until the chocolate has melted and the custard is smooth. Refrigerate the custard until needed.

3 Serve hot or cold with poached fruit, if desired.

Janelle's Favourite Mud Cake

I have consumed many mud cakes in my time and I assure you that this is one of the best – and it improves in flavour if it is allowed to stand.

SERVES: *8–10*

PREPARATION TIME:
20 minutes

COOKING TIME:
1½ hours

The strong black coffee in this recipe is brewed or plunger coffee. Instant coffee powder can be used provided it is mixed with water. I recommend 2 teaspoons of coffee powder to ¼ cup of water.

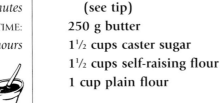

Place the chocolate, coffee and butter in a large heatproof bowl and heat, uncovered, stirring every minute, for 3–4 minutes on MEDIUM–HIGH/ *650 watts/70%.*

Place the chocolate in a clean, dry heatproof bowl and heat, uncovered, for 2–3 minutes on MEDIUM/*500 watts/ 50%, stirring every minute.*

200 g cooking chocolate
1½ cups very strong black coffee
   (see tip)
250 g butter
1½ cups caster sugar
1½ cups self-raising flour
1 cup plain flour

¼ cup cocoa
2 eggs
1 teaspoon vanilla essence

ICING

200 g cooking chocolate
3 tablespoons sour cream

1   Preheat the oven to 150°C (300° F). Grease a 23-cm round or square cake tin and line with non-stick baking paper.

2   Place the chocolate, coffee and butter in a medium saucepan, and cook over medium heat, stirring constantly, until the chocolate and butter have melted and the mixture is smooth. (Alternatively, see the first microwave tip.)

3   Remove the chocolate and butter mixture from the heat and transfer to a large bowl. Cool the chocolate mixture slightly and add the sugar, mixing well.

4   Sift together the self-raising flour, plain flour and cocoa. Whisk the dry ingredients into the chocolate mixture. Add the eggs and vanilla essence, whisking well to ensure a smooth batter. (The mixture will be quite runny.) Pour the batter into the prepared tin and bake for 1 hour 10 minutes– 1½ hours, or until the cake has come away from the sides of the tin. Allow the cake to cool for 15 minutes in the tin before turning it out onto a wire rack to cool. (Don't worry if the cake cracks – mud cakes often crack due to their high sugar content.) Ice the cake when the cake is cold.

5   *ICING*   Place the chocolate in a heatproof bowl over a saucepan of simmering water, stirring constantly until the chocolate has melted. (Alternatively, see the second microwave tip.) Remove the chocolate from the heat and stir in the sour cream, mixing well.

Best-ever Rum Balls

This recipe is from Ella Douthie, who is 70 years young. I have never tasted a rum ball that even comes close to these delectable morsels. Thanks, Ella!

MAKES: *24*
PREPARATION TIME:
20 minutes
CHILLING TIME:
3 days

Rum balls may also be coated in grated white or milk chocolate.

Rum balls should be served at room temperature.

250 g Marie biscuits
1 cup icing sugar
2 tablespoons NESTLÉ Baking Cocoa
2 tablespoons golden syrup
4 tablespoons Bundaberg Rum
2 tablespoons sweet cooking sherry

pinch of salt
200 g PLAISTOWE Cooking Chocolate, grated or chocolate sprinkles

1. Place the biscuits in the bowl of a food processor and process to fine crumbs. Transfer the crumbs to a large mixing bowl.

2. Add the icing sugar, cocoa, golden syrup, rum, sherry and salt. Mix the ingredients well, adding more rum, if necessary, to make a suitable consistency for rolling.

3. Roll the mixture into walnut-sized balls, using moist hands.

4. Drop six balls at a time into a bag containing the grated chocolate or chocolate sprinkles, and shake, making sure all the rum balls are well coated. Place the coated rum balls in a container lined with non-stick baking paper, then cover and chill in the refrigerator for a few days. The flavour of the rum balls improves the longer they are chilled.

Failproof Hot Chocolate Soufflé

Soufflés are often taboo as far as home cooks are concerned. This is a failproof method, provided you follow my tips.

MAKES: 6
PREPARATION TIME:
10 minutes
COOKING TIME:
25 minutes

30 g melted butter and 2 tablespoons sugar (to prepare soufflé dishes)	4 egg yolks
	¼ cup caster sugar
	6 egg whites
185 g cooking chocolate	pinch of cream of tartar
185 g butter	icing sugar, for dusting

Use large eggs (size 61g) when making this soufflé. The soufflé can be prepared to the end of step 3, 4–6 hours beforehand. Cover the mixture with wrap and leave at room temperature.

Place the chocolate and butter in a large heatproof bowl. Cook the chocolate mixture, uncovered, stirring every minute, for 2–3 minutes on MEDIUM-HIGH/650 watts/70%.

1. Brush 6 × 1-cup capacity soufflé dishes or heatproof mugs with the melted butter. Coat the base and sides of the dishes or mugs with the sugar (this assists the soufflé to climb up the dish and rise). Place the prepared dishes on a baking tray (this makes it easy to get the soufflés in and out of the oven quickly).

2. Combine the chocolate and the butter in a small saucepan. Cook over a low heat, stirring constantly, until the chocolate has melted and the sauce is smooth. (Alternatively, see the microwave tip.) Remove the chocolate sauce from the heat and transfer to a large bowl. (If you are heavy-handed and are beginning to lack confidence in your ability to make a soufflé, add 1 tablespoon of self-raising flour to the chocolate mixture.)

3. Use an electric mixer to mix the egg yolks and 1 tablespoon of the caster sugar together until pale in colour. Add the egg and sugar mixture to the warm chocolate mixture and stir well.

4. Just before serving, preheat the oven to 200°C (390°F). Use an electric mixer to beat the egg whites with the cream of tartar until soft peaks form. Gradually add the remaining sugar to the egg whites, mixing until the sugar has dissolved. Fold ⅓ of the egg white and sugar mixture into the chocolate mixture. As gently as possible, fold in the remaining egg white mixture. Spoon the chocolate soufflé mixture into the prepared dishes. Place in the oven and bake for 15–18 minutes, or until the soufflés are well risen. Serve immediately, dusted with icing sugar.

Fudge Brownie Cookies

These cookies are moist, chocolatey, irresistible and store really well.

MAKES: *36*
PREPARATION TIME:
*10 minutes, plus
chilling time*
COOKING TIME:
12 minutes

*Cookies will be soft
to touch after
baking, but will firm
on cooling.*

*Place the butter and
chocolate in a
heatproof bowl.
Heat, uncovered,
stirring every
minute, for
2–3 minutes on*
MEDIUM–HIGH/
*650 watts/70% or
until smooth.*

125 g butter
200 g cooking chocolate
2 eggs
¾ cup brown sugar

1 cup plain flour
½ cup cocoa
½ cup desiccated coconut
1 cup Nestlé White Choc Bits

1 Preheat the oven to 180°C (350°F). Grease 3 baking trays and line them with non-stick baking paper.

2 Place the butter and chocolate in a saucepan, and cook, stirring constantly, over a medium–low heat until the butter and chocolate have melted and are smooth. (Alternatively, see the microwave tip.) Remove the chocolate mixture from the heat, then transfer it to a large bowl and allow to cool.

3 Add the eggs and brown sugar and mix well. Sift the flour and cocoa and fold them into the chocolate mixture with the coconut and white Choc Bits.

4 Roll one tablespoon of the cookie mixture into a ball. Repeat until all the mixture has been used. Place the balls onto the prepared trays. Flatten the cookies with a fork. Place the trays in the oven and bake for 12 minutes. Allow the cookies to cool for 5 minutes on the trays before transferring to a wire rack to cool.

OPPOSITE: Fudge Brownie Cookies (left) and Best-ever Choc-chip Cookies (see page 58).

➤

Best-ever Choc-chip Cookies

Calling anything 'best-ever' is a big call! I like cookies to be a little fudgy in the centre and these certainly are.

MAKES: *24*
PREPARATION TIME:
15 minutes
COOKING TIME:
14 minutes

If you like your cookies soft and fudgy in the centre, cook them for 12 minutes only.

1 egg
1 cup brown sugar
1 teaspoon vanilla essence
½ cup canola oil

¾ cup self-raising flour
¾ cup plain flour
1 cup Nestlé Dark Choc Bits

1 Preheat the oven to 180°C (350°F). Grease 2 baking trays and line them with non-stick baking paper.

2 Combine the egg, brown sugar, vanilla essence and oil in a large bowl. Sift in the flours and add the dark Choc Bits, mixing until well combined.

3 Roll 1 tablespoonful of the mixture into a ball. Repeat until all the dough is used. Place the balls on the prepared baking trays, then slightly flatten them with a fork.

4 Place the cookies in the oven and bake for 12–14 minutes, or until golden in colour. Allow the cookies to stand on the trays for 5 minutes before transferring them to a wire rack to cool. (See photograph opposite page 56.)

Classic Marshmallow Cocoa

SERVES: 4

PREPARATION TIME:
10 minutes

COOKING TIME:
5 minutes

Why not try dipping a teaspoon or a cinnamon stick in melted dark melts, allowing the chocolate to set, then using the teaspoon or cinnamon stick to stir the Classic Marshmallow Cocoa?

Whisk the cocoa, water and sugar in a microwave-safe jug. Add the milk. Cook the chocolate milk, uncovered, whisking every minute, for 4–5 minutes on HIGH/800 watts/ 100%.

100 g milk chocolate melts, melted
4 tablespoons cocoa
1 tablespoon boiling water
sugar, to taste

750 ml milk
marshmallows
extra cocoa, for dusting

1. Spread the milk melts onto a baking tray and allow to set. Drag a sharp knife over the milk melts to make chocolate curls.

2. Whisk the cocoa with the water and sugar in a medium bowl. Add the milk. Transfer the chocolate milk to a medium saucepan and bring just to boiling point, stirring often. Remove the milk from the heat immediately bubbles begin to form (do not allow the milk to boil). (Alternatively, see the microwave tip.)

3. Carefully pour the cocoa into 4 cups, top with the marshmallows and chocolate curls, then dust with the cocoa. Serve immediately. (See photograph opposite page 60.)

Fudge Brownie Muffins

While I was in Tasmania in 1996, I tasted the best chocolate muffin ever. I have tried to recreate the recipe here.

MAKES: *12*

PREPARATION TIME:
15 minutes

COOKING TIME:
20 minutes

If you have any muffins left over they can be warmed by placing them on a microwave-safe plate and heating them, uncovered, for 1–3 minutes on MEDIUM/500 watts/ *50%, depending on the quantity.*

Place the dark melts and cream into a heatproof bowl. Heat, uncovered, stirring twice, for 1½–2 minutes on MEDIUM–HIGH/ *650 watts/70%.*

100 g dark chocolate melts
¼ cup pouring or thickened cream
1¼ cups self-raising flour
½ cup cocoa
1 cup caster sugar
½ cup pouring or thickened cream, extra

2 eggs
1 teaspoon vanilla essence
3 tablespoons vegetable oil (such as canola oil)
12 large paper patty cases

1   Preheat the oven to 200°C (390°F). Place the patty cases into 1 × 12 (⅓-cup capacity) muffin tray.

2   Combine the dark melts and cream in a small saucepan. Stir constantly over a low heat until the chocolate has melted and the sauce is smooth. (Alternatively, see the microwave tip.) Set the chocolate mixture aside to cool and thicken.

3   Sift the flour and cocoa into a large bowl. Add the sugar and mix to combine the ingredients.

4   Combine the extra cream, eggs, vanilla essence and oil. Gently fold the wet ingredients into the dry ingredients until just combined. (The mixture will be quite thick.) Add the cooled chocolate mixture and swirl carefully through the muffin batter. Do not overmix. Spoon the batter into the prepared patty cases.

5   Place in the oven and bake for 17–20 minutes or until well-risen and firm to touch. Allow to cool for a few minutes. Remember: muffins should always be eaten warm, so serve them immediately.

OPPOSITE: Fudge Brownie Muffins and Classic Marshmallow Cocoa (see page 59).

➤

Milk Chocolate Creme Caramel

I made this dessert for one of my regular cooking segments on television, only to have it demolished in record time. And it is still being talked about!

SERVES: 6–8
PREPARATION TIME:
40 minutes/
20 minutes in the
microwave
COOKING TIME:
45 minutes/
30 minutes in the
microwave

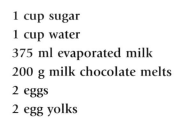

The inclusion of milk melts in this recipe not only adds flavour, but it also ensures the Creme Caramel will always set.

1 cup sugar
1 cup water
375 ml evaporated milk
200 g milk chocolate melts
2 eggs
2 egg yolks

¹⁄₃ cup caster sugar
¹⁄₄ teaspoon vanilla essence
300 ml pure cream
chocolate-dipped strawberries and
    chocolate sticks (see page 6), to
    serve

1   Preheat the oven to 150°C (300°F). Lightly grease a 20-cm round heatproof container or cake tin.

2   Place the sugar and water in a small saucepan and cook over a medium heat. Stir constantly until the sugar has dissolved (the liquid will be clear). Stop stirring and allow the syrup to come to the boil. Turn the heat down to low and allow the syrup to simmer until a light gold colour – approximately 25–30 minutes. Remove from heat immediately. Carefully pour the hot caramel into the prepared dish and allow it to set.

3   Meanwhile, in a separate saucepan combine the evaporated milk and the milk melts. Stir the mixture constantly over a medium heat until the chocolate has melted and is smooth. Remove the chocolate mixture from the heat.

4   Whisk the eggs, egg yolks, caster sugar and vanilla essence until well combined. Add the chocolate mixture and cream. Mix thoroughly. Pour the chocolate mixture over the cooled caramel. Place the container into a baking dish. Pour in enough warm water to come halfway up the sides of the baking dish (this is known as a water bath). Place the baking dish in the oven and bake, uncovered, for 40–45 minutes. Allow the creme caramel to cool slightly in the water bath before removing it. Cover and refrigerate overnight, for at least 12 hours.

5   Carefully run a flat-bladed knife around the edge of the creme caramel. Turn it out onto a serving platter and decorate with chocolate-dipped strawberries and chocolate sticks, if desired.

MICROWAVE INSTRUCTIONS
● Place the sugar and water in a heatproof and microwave-safe jug. Heat, uncovered, for 2 minutes on HIGH/800 watts/100%. Stir well to ensure that the sugar has dissolved. Place back in the microwave and cook for ➤

17–20 minutes, uncovered, without stirring, until the syrup turns a light golden colour. Pour into the base of a heatproof, microwave-safe 20-cm round container.

- Allow the caramel to cool and thicken.
- Place the evaporated milk and milk melts in a small heatproof and microwave-safe bowl. Heat, uncovered, for 3–4 minutes on MEDIUM–HIGH/650 watts/70%, then stir until the milk and chocolate are combined.
- Whisk the eggs, egg yolks, caster sugar, and vanilla essence until well combined. Add the chocolate mixture and cream. Mix thoroughly. Pour the mixture over the cooled caramel. Place the creme caramel into a deep pie plate, and pour in enough warm water to come halfway up the sides of the dish (this is known as a water bath).
- Cook, uncovered, for 24–30 minutes on MEDIUM–LOW/350 watts/30%. The centre will still be slightly wobbly; this will firm on chilling. Cover with aluminium foil and allow the creme caramel to cool. Refrigerate the creme caramel overnight.

Chocolate Ganache

MAKES: ³/₄ *cup*

PREPARATION TIME:
*5 minutes, plus
standing time*

COOKING TIME:
5 minutes

*Place the chocolate
and butter in a
heatproof bowl.
Heat, uncovered,
ring every minute,
or 3–4 minutes on
EDIUM/500 watts/
50%.*

200 g cooking chocolate   200 g butter

1   Place the chocolate and butter in a small saucepan. Cook over low heat, stirring constantly, until the chocolate and butter have melted and the mixture is smooth. (Alternatively, see the microwave tip.) Remove the melted chocolate mixture from the heat and transfer to a bowl. Allow to stand at room temperature, stirring from time to time, until the mixture becomes firm enough to work with.

Chocolate Sauce

MAKES: 1¼ *cups*

PREPARATION TIME:
5 minutes

COOKING TIME:
5 minutes

*Place the chocolate
and cream in a
heatproof bowl or
. Heat, uncovered,
ring every minute,
or 2–3 minutes on
EDIUM/500 watts/
50%.*

200 g cooking chocolate   ½ cup pouring or thickened cream

1   Place the chocolate and cream into a small saucepan and cook over a low heat. Stir constantly until the chocolate melts and the sauce is smooth. (Alternatively, see the microwave tip.) This sauce will keep in an airtight container for 10 days in the refrigerator.

Chocolate Icing 1

MAKES: *1¹/₂ cups*
PREPARATION TIME:
5 minutes

100 g butter, softened
125 g cooking chocolate or dark
    chocolate melts, melted

1 cup icing sugar

_1_ Beat the butter and chocolate until well combined. Add the icing sugar and mix to a smooth consistency. Spread the mixture quickly over cakes, slices, or biscuits. The icing will set almost immediately. The quantity this recipe makes is sufficient to ice the top and sides of a 20-cm cake.

Chocolate Icing 2

MAKES: *1 cup*
PREPARATION TIME: *5 minutes*
COOKING TIME:
30 seconds

1¹/₂ cups icing sugar
3 tablespoons cocoa

1 tablespoon butter, softened
boiling water

_1_ Sift the icing sugar and cocoa into a medium bowl. Add the butter and enough boiling water to form a very thick paste. Place the bowl over a saucepan of boiling water and stir until the mixture has softened slightly. (Alternatively, see the microwave tip.) Spread the mixture quickly over cakes, slices, or biscuits. The icing will set almost immediately. The quantity this recipe makes is sufficient to ice the top and sides of a 20-cm cake.

Place the icing sugar, cocoa and butter in a medium heatproof bowl. Add enough boiling water to form a very thick paste. Place the bowl in the microwave and heat for 30 seconds on HIGH/*800 watts/ 100%.*

Sweet Treats

Chocolate is one of life's pleasures; another is eating out and tasting one of the chef's special creations. Years ago I tasted a honeycomb ice-cream cake; it was simply unforgettable. This and working with Nestlé on occasions gave me the idea to develop recipes using some of the very popular confectionery we all know and love. I suggest you try them all, but the wicked Soft-centred Muffins, and the Cream Cheese Choc Wafer Slice were favourites among my taste-testers.

Macadamia Chocky Rock

MAKES: 24

PREPARATION TIME:
10 minutes

CHILLING TIME:
2–3 hours

An easy way to cut marshmallows is to dip a pair of scissors into cornflour and snip them in half.

2 × 375 g milk chocolate melts, melted
250 g white and pink marshmallows, halved

1 cup macadamia nuts, toasted and roughly chopped

1. Line a 28 × 18-cm lamington tin with non-stick baking paper.

2. In a large bowl, combine the milk melts, marshmallows and nuts, and mix until just combined.

3. Spread the mixture into the prepared tin. Cover the chocky rock and refrigerate for 2–3 hours, or until firm.

4. Cut the chocky rock into squares using a warm knife.

White Rocky Road Cups

Thank you Heather James of Bonython for allowing me to print this recipe. It is an absolute hit with everyone who tries it.

MAKES: 36

PREPARATION TIME:
10 minutes

COOKING TIME:
2–3 minutes

CHILLING TIME:
1 hour

375 g white chocolate melts, melted
200 g Allen's Jelly Tots
1½ cups Rice Bubbles

2 cups mini marshmallows
36 paper patty cases

1. Combine all the ingredients thoroughly, then spoon the rocky road mixture into the patty cases.

2. Refrigerate until set, approximately 1 hour.

OPPOSITE: Macadamia Chocky Rock (left) and White Rocky Road Cups (this page).

➤

Double-dipped Strawberries

MAKES:
approximately 36
PREPARATION TIME: 5
minutes
COOKING TIME:
25–35 minutes

Place the sugar and water in a medium heatproof bowl or jug. Heat the syrup, uncovered, for 3–4 minutes on HIGH/ 800 watts/100%. Remove the syrup from the microwave and stir to ensure all the sugar has dissolved, brushing down any sugar crystals that have formed on the edges with a wet pastry brush. Return the syrup to the microwave, and cook, uncovered, for 15–20 minutes on HIGH/800 watts/ 100%, or until golden.

1 cup white sugar
²/₃ cup water
500 g strawberries

200 g dark, milk or white chocolate melts, melted

1. Place the sugar and water in a small saucepan and cook over medium heat, stirring until the sugar has dissolved. (The liquid will be clear.) Increase heat and allow the syrup to come to the boil. Do not stir the syrup. Reduce heat to low and allow the syrup to simmer until it is golden, approximately 25–30 minutes. Use a wet pastry brush to brush down any sugar crystals that appear on the side of the saucepan. (Alternatively, see the microwave tip.)

2. Meanwhile, press the strawberries onto the ends of wooden skewers. Carefully dip each one into the hot caramel. Allow the caramel to set on a tray lined with non-stick baking paper.

3. Half dip the toffee strawberries in the melted chocolate. Allow the chocolate to set, then serve immediately as toffee fruit will not hold up for a long time (especially on humid days).

Chocolate Coconut Crunchies

These are really moreish treats. Once you have eaten one, it is easy to polish off many more – I speak from experience!

MAKES: *18*
PREPARATION TIME:
10 minutes
COOKING TIME:
5 minutes
SETTING TIME:
1 hour

8 × 20 g Nestlé Golden Rough, roughly chopped
200 g milk chocolate melts

4 tablespoons peanut butter
100 g fried egg noodles
18 paper patty cases

1 Combine the Golden Rough, milk melts and peanut butter in a medium saucepan. Cook over a low heat, stirring constantly, until the chocolate has melted and the mixture is well combined. (Alternatively, see the microwave tip.) Remove from the heat and allow the chocolate mixture to cool slightly.

Combine the Golden Rough, milk melts and peanut butter in a medium heatproof bowl. Heat the chocolate mixture, uncovered, for 4–5 minutes on MEDIUM/500 watts/50%, stirring every minute until well combined.

2 Stir in the noodles and mix until they are well coated with the chocolate mixture.

3 Spoon the chocolate-coated noodles into paper patty cases and allow to set, approximately 1 hour.

Chocolate Snakes

MAKES:
approximately 36
PREPARATION TIME:
15 minutes
COOKING TIME:
3 minutes
SETTING TIME:
20 minutes

125 g dark chocolate melts

2 × 180 g Allen's Snakes Alive

1 Line 2 baking trays with non-stick baking paper.

2 Place the dark melts in a heatproof bowl on top of a pan of simmering water. Make sure that the water does not touch the base of the bowl. Stir the dark melts constantly until the chocolate has melted. Remove the melted chocolate from the heat.

3 Take one snake at a time and dip half the snake into the chocolate. Place the chocolate-dipped snakes on the prepared tray to set, approximately 20 minutes.

OPPOSITE: Chocolate Coconut Crunchies and Chocolate Snakes (this page).

➤

Peanut Toffee Pavlova

SERVES: *8–10*
PREPARATION TIME:
20 minutes
COOKING TIME:
2 hours

4 egg whites
½ teaspoon cream of tartar
1 cup caster sugar
3 tablespoons cornflour
6 teaspoons cocoa

1 teaspoon white vinegar
2 × 40 g Nestlé Scorched Peanut
   Bar, chopped
300 ml thickened cream, whipped
mixed berries of choice

Do not spread the pavlova out too widely on the tray as it will naturally flatten while baking.

If you require an evenly shaped pavlova, place a 20-cm springform tin onto the baking tray and line the sides with baking paper, then spoon the pavlova mixture into the tin and cook.

Do not top the pavlova with cream until just before serving as it may collapse.

1 Preheat the oven to 125°C (250°F). Grease and line a baking tray with non-stick baking paper. Trace a 20-cm circle in the middle of the paper.

2 Using an electric mixer, beat the egg whites with the cream of tartar until soft peaks form. Gradually add the sugar a tablespoon at a time and beat until the sugar has dissolved and the mixture is thick and glossy.

3 Fold in the combined sifted cornflour and cocoa, vinegar and one Scorched Peanut Bar. Spoon the mixture into the circle on the prepared tray, piling it up.

4 Bake for 1½–2 hours or until the pavlova is dry and crisp (if the pavlova starts to brown a little, turn the oven down to 100°C/210°F). Allow to cool in the oven.

5 Prior to serving, place the pavlova onto a serving platter. Top with whipped cream, berries and the extra chopped Scorched Peanut Bar. Serve immediately.

Quick Mix Fudge Cake

SERVES: *8–10*

PREPARATION TIME:
15 minutes

COOKING TIME:
55 minutes

Place the dark melts and butter in a large heatproof bowl. Heat, uncovered, for 1–2 minutes on MEDIUM–HIGH/650 *watts/70%, or until melted. Stir the mixture well.*

CAKE

1 cup self-raising flour
²/₃ cup caster sugar
250 g dark chocolate melts
125 g butter
¹/₃ cup cocoa
¹/₂ cup boiling water
3 eggs

ICING

100 g butter, softened
125 g cooking chocolate, melted
³/₄ cup icing sugar

2 × 50 g Nestlé Rolo,
1 × 45 g Nestlé Kit Kat,
1 × 50 g Nestlé Smarties,
2 × 50 g Nestlé Violet Crumble
and 200 g Allen's Jelly Tots, for
decoration

1. Preheat the oven to 160°C (315°F). Grease a 20-cm square cake tin and line with non-stick baking paper.

2. *CAKE* Sift the flour into a large bowl, then stir in the sugar.

3. Melt the dark melts and butter in a medium saucepan over a low heat, stirring constantly, until the mixture is well combined. (Alternatively, see the microwave tip.) Remove the chocolate mixture from the heat and allow it to cool slightly.

4. Combine the cocoa and water in a small bowl, mixing until well combined. Add the cocoa mixture and the eggs to the chocolate mixture. Mix until smooth using a whisk. Add this chocolate mixture to the dry ingredients and whisk until the batter is smooth and well combined.

5. Pour the batter into the prepared tin, place in the oven and bake for 45–50 minutes, or until the cake is cooked when tested with a skewer. (Insert a skewer into the centre of the cake; if it comes out clean, the cake is cooked.) Allow the cake to cool for 10 minutes in the tin before turning it out onto a wire rack to cool.

6. *ICING* Beat the butter and chocolate until well combined. Add the icing sugar and mix to a smooth consistency.

7. Spread the cake with the icing and decorate with the sweets.

Chocolate Ice-cream Cones

MAKES: *12*
PREPARATION TIME:
*30 minutes plus
setting time*
COOKING TIME:
*10 minutes/2
minutes in the
microwave*
SETTING TIME:
*overnight plus
30 minutes*

*Place the dark melts
in a clean, dry heat-
resistant bowl. Heat,
uncovered, stirring
after each minute,
for 2 minutes on
MEDIUM–HIGH/650
watts/70% until
smooth.*

1 litre vanilla ice-cream, slightly
  softened
250 g Nestlé Dark Choc Bits
200 g dark chocolate melts

12 sugar cones
100 g milk or white chocolate
  melts, melted

1   Mix the dark Choc Bits through the ice-cream. Place back into the ice-cream container. Place in the freezer to reset overnight.

2   Gather 12 bottles with thin necks (making sure that the ice-cream cones will fit upside-down over the necks).

3   Place the dark melts in a large heatproof bowl over a saucepan of simmering water. Make sure that the water does not touch the base of the bowl. Stir constantly until the chocolate has melted, approximately 5–6 minutes. (Alternatively, see the microwave tip.) Remove the bowl from the heat. Use a clean, dry pastry brush to brush each cone with the melted chocolate, making sure a little of the base is left uncovered. Turn upside-down over the bottle and allow to set, approximately 20 minutes.

4   Place the milk melts or white melts in a clean, dry heatproof bowl, and melt as for the dark melts. Spoon the chocolate into a corner of a storage bag. Cut off the corner with a pair of sharp scissors. Drizzle the melted chocolate all over the cone and allow to set, approximately 10 minutes.

5   Wrap the base of each cone in a napkin or in plastic wrap. Scoop some of the choc chip ice-cream into each cone and enjoy.

Caramel Oat Wedges

This recipe has been given the nod by everyone who has sampled it, including Christa from Peter's of Kensington.

MAKES: *8–10*

PREPARATION TIME:
10 minutes

COOKING TIME:
20–25 minutes

125 g butter
2 tablespoons golden syrup
½ teaspoon bicarbonate of soda
2 tablespoons boiling water
1½ cups rolled oats

½ cup caster sugar
¾ cup desiccated coconut
1 cup plain flour, sifted
2 × 60 g Nestlé Chokito, roughly
    chopped

Place the butter and golden syrup in a large heatproof, microwave-safe bowl. Heat the caramel mixture, uncovered, for 2½–3 minutes on MEDIUM–HIGH/650 *watts/70%, or until the mixture is very hot.*

1   Preheat the oven to 160°C (315°F). Grease a 20-cm round cake tin and line with non-stick baking paper.

2   Combine the butter and golden syrup in a small saucepan. Cook over medium heat, stirring constantly, until the butter has melted and the mixture is very hot. (Alternatively, see the microwave tip.) Remove the caramel from the heat and stir in the combined bicarbonate of soda and water. The mixture will become frothy. Transfer the caramel mixture to a large mixing bowl. Cool slightly.

3   Add the rolled oats, sugar, coconut and flour, and mix well. Stir in the Chokito and mix until the ingredients are well combined.

4   Press the mixture into the prepared tin. Place the tin in the oven and bake for 20–25 minutes, or until golden. The cake is cooked when a skewer inserted in the centre comes out clean. Allow to cool in the tin.

5   Turn out the cake and cut into wedges before serving.

Soft-centred Muffins

When my nieces and nephews tried these muffins, the comment was 'Nell you're the best cooker'.

MAKES: *24 mini muffins or 12 large muffins*
PREPARATION TIME: *10 minutes*
COOKING TIME: *12–15 minutes*

With this recipe the Rolo melts in the centre and becomes very hot, so allow the muffins to cool a little before serving.

2 cups self-raising flour
¼ cup cocoa
½ cup brown sugar
125 g butter, melted
2 eggs

1 cup milk
3 × 50 g Nestlé Rolo

icing sugar, for dusting (optional)

1 Preheat the oven to 200°C (390°F). Grease 2 × 12 mini muffin trays (⅛-cup capacity) or 2 × 6 muffin trays (⅓-cup capacity).

2 Sift the flour and cocoa into a large bowl. Add the brown sugar and mix to combine.

3 Mix the butter, eggs and milk together, then fold into the dry ingredients until just combined.

4 Spoon half the muffin mixture into the prepared trays. Place 2 individual Rolo chocolates in the centre of each muffin, then top with the remaining muffin mixture.

5 Place the muffins in the oven and bake for 12–15 minutes, or until cooked. Serve warm with icing sugar, if desired.

Cream Cheese Choc Wafer Slice

The idea for this recipe was inspired by Phil and Julie from Channel 9's 'What's Cooking'.

MAKES: *24*
PREPARATION TIME: *25 minutes plus chilling time*
CHILLING TIME: *overnight plus 1 hour*

3 × 90 g Nestlé Kit Kat, crushed
50 g butter, melted
375 g cream cheese, softened
grated rind of 1 orange
⅓ cup caster sugar
200 g cooking chocolate, melted

250 g shortbread biscuits, roughly broken
2 × 40 g Nestlé Scorched Peanut Bar, roughly chopped
icing sugar or cocoa, for dusting

Place wooden skewers across the top of the slice and dust with icing sugar or cocoa. Carefully lift skewers to obtain a pattern.

Scotch Finger biscuits may be used instead of shortbread.

1 Grease a 28 × 18-cm lamington tin and line with non-stick baking paper.

2 Combine the crushed Kit Kat and butter, mixing well. Press the mixture into the prepared tin (this is a little fiddly but worth the trouble) and refrigerate for 1 hour.

3 Beat the cream cheese, orange rind and caster sugar until light and fluffy. Add the chocolate and mix until well combined. Fold in the biscuits and Scorched Peanut Bars, mixing until all are well coated.

4 Spread the chocolate mixture evenly over the Kit Kat base. Cover and chill overnight.

5 Decorate with the icing sugar or cocoa and cut the slice into squares.

Honeycomb Cheesecake

There is only one word for this recipe – delicious!

SERVES: *8*

PREPARATION TIME:
20 minutes

COOKING TIME:
*1 hour/15–18
minutes in the
microwave*

*If you want
the cheesecake
turned out after
microwaving, you
can use a deep
20-cm round
heatproof pie plate,
lined with non-stick
baking paper. After
the cheesecake has
cooled, run a flat-
bladed knife around
the edges and loosely
cover the top with a
layer of plastic wrap.
Turn the cheesecake
out onto a board,
remove the paper
lining and flip the
cheesecake onto a
serving plate.*

BASE

175 g shredded wheatmeal biscuits
100 g butter, melted
1 teaspoon ground nutmeg

FILLING

500 g cream cheese, softened
²/₃ cup caster sugar
grated rind of 1 lemon

1 tablespoon lemon juice
2 eggs
1½ cups pouring cream
2 × 50 g Nestlé Violet Crumble

1. Preheat the oven to 160°C (315°F). Lightly grease a 20-cm springform cake tin.

2. *BASE* Process the biscuits to fine crumbs in a food processor. Add the butter and nutmeg and mix well. Press the biscuit base into the prepared tin and chill until the filling is ready.

3. *FILLING* Use an electric mixer to beat the cream cheese, sugar and lemon rind together until light and creamy. Add the lemon juice and eggs, one at a time, mixing well after each addition.

4. Fold in ½ cup of the cream and one Violet Crumble, roughly chopped. Pour the filling over the prepared base.

5. Place the cake tin on a baking tray and transfer to the oven. Bake the cheesecake for about 1 hour, or until it is cooked when a skewer inserted into the centre of the cheesecake comes out clean. (Do not be concerned if the cheesecake cracks on top – this is due to the honeycomb.) Allow the cheesecake to cool in the tin.

6. To serve, whip the remaining cream and spread it evenly over the top of the cheesecake. Decorate with the remaining Violet Crumble, roughly chopped.

MICROWAVE INSTRUCTIONS
- Lightly grease a 20-cm deep round heatproof pie plate.
- Process the biscuits to fine crumbs in the food processor. Add the butter and nutmeg and mix well. Press the biscuit base into the prepared container and chill until the filling is ready. ➤

- Use an electric mixer to beat the cream cheese, sugar and lemon rind together until light and creamy. Add the lemon juice and eggs, one at a time, mixing well after each addition.
- Fold in $1/2$ cup of the cream and one Violet Crumble, roughly chopped. Pour the filling over the prepared base.
- Place the cheesecake onto a microwave-safe rack and cook, uncovered, for 15–18 minutes on MEDIUM/500 watts/50%. Allow the cheesecake to stand; the centre will firm on standing. (Do not be concerned if the cheesecake cracks on top – this is due to the honeycomb.) Allow the cheesecake to cool in the container.

A Hint of Chocolate

I don't know many people who don't like chocolate, but not every occasion calls for a 'Death by Chocolate' hit. Many of the recipes in this chapter include fresh fruit, which is the dominating flavour, like Mango and White Chocolate Frozen Yoghurt, Upside-down Peach and Hazelnut Cake or Flourless Orange and Almond Cake. These are all matches made in heaven; they utilise chocolate sparingly, but the results are dazzling.

Upside-down Peach and Hazelnut Cake

SERVES: 8

PREPARATION TIME:
25 minutes

COOKING TIME:
*40 minutes/
12 minutes in the
microwave*

*When fresh peaches
are not in season,
canned peaches can
be used. Make sure
they are drained
well on a paper
towel first.*

BASE
60 g butter
½ cup brown sugar
2–3 large free-stone peaches, sliced

CAKE
100 g butter
½ cup caster sugar
1 teaspoon vanilla essence
2 eggs
125 g white chocolate melts,
    melted
⅓ cup ground toasted hazelnuts

1¼ cups self-raising flour, sifted
2 tablespoons cocoa
⅓ cup peach nectar

pure cream, to serve (optional)
extra peaches, to serve (optional)

1   Preheat the oven to 180°C (350°F). Grease a 20-cm round cake tin and line it with non-stick baking paper.

2   *BASE*   Place the butter and brown sugar in a small saucepan and cook over medium heat, stirring constantly, until the butter has melted and the mixture is smooth. Spread the mixture evenly over the base of the prepared tin.

3   Arrange the peaches decoratively over the butter and sugar base.

4   *CAKE*   Cream the butter, sugar and vanilla essence until light and fluffy. Add the eggs one at a time, beating well after each addition. Fold in the white melts, hazelnuts, flour, cocoa and peach nectar. (The batter will be very thick.) Spread the batter carefully over the peaches.

5   Place the cake in the oven and bake for 35–40 minutes, or until a skewer inserted in the centre of the cake comes out clean. Allow the cake to stand for 10 minutes in the tin before turning out onto a serving platter.

6   Serve the cake warm with pure cream and extra peaches, if desired.

Microwave Cherry Jam Muffins

*During summer, with its abundance of fruit, I make jam in the microwave
constantly – it really is quick, easy and delicious.*

MAKES: *12*

PREPARATION TIME:
*40 minutes
(includes making
jam)*

COOKING TIME:
25 minutes

*When sterilising jars
make sure they have
metal lids. Wash the
jars and lids in hot
soapy water and
then rinse well in
hot clean water.
Place into a large
saucepan or stock
pot of boiling water
and simmer for
10 minutes. Remove
the jars and lids
and place onto a
baking tray in a
preheated oven for
15 minutes at
150°C (300°F) or
until completely dry.
Always fill hot jars
with hot jam; cover
lightly with a clean
tea towel until cooled.
Seal and label when
jam is cold.*

MICROWAVE CHERRY JAM

**500 g fresh cherries, pitted and
 halved**

³/₄ cup caster sugar

¹/₂ cup lemon juice

MUFFINS

2 cups self-raising flour

¹/₂ cup cocoa

1¹/₄ cups caster sugar

125 g butter, melted

³/₄ cup buttermilk

2 eggs

icing sugar, for dusting
whipped cream, to serve (optional)

1   MICROWAVE CHERRY JAM   Place the cherries, sugar and lemon juice in a
3-litre heatproof bowl. Cook, uncovered, in the microwave for 5 minutes on
HIGH/800 watts/100%. Remove the bowl from the microwave, stir and place
the bowl back into the microwave and cook, stirring every 5 minutes, for a
further 20–25 minutes or until the jam has set. (Use the saucer test to check
that the jam has set by placing a saucer in the freezer for 5 minutes. Remove
the chilled saucer from the freezer and drop 1–2 teaspoons of jam onto it.
Place back in the freezer for 2–3 minutes. Lightly touch the jam with your
finger. If a skin has formed that wrinkles when you touch it, the jam has set
and is ready to bottle; if not, cook a few minutes longer and check again.)
Spoon the jam into warm sterilised jars and allow to cool. Seal and label.

2   Preheat the oven to 180°C (350°F). Grease 2 × 6 (¹/₃-cup capacity) muffin
trays.

3   MUFFINS   Sift the flour and cocoa into a large bowl. Add the sugar and mix
until combined.

4   In a separate bowl, combine the butter, buttermilk and eggs, then fold this
mixture into the dry ingredients, being careful not to over mix. Spoon half the
mixture into the prepared tin, then place a spoonful of jam into the centre of
each muffin. Top with the remaining muffin mixture.

5   Bake for 20–25 minutes or until cooked. Dust with icing sugar and serve hot
with extra jam and whipped cream, if desired.

Mango and White Chocolate Frozen Yoghurt

I found myself making this frozen dessert many times last summer as it so refreshing and delicious.

SERVES: 6–8

PREPARATION TIME:
30 minutes plus freezing time

COOKING TIME:
10 minutes

FREEZING TIME:
8–12 hours

Place the white melts and cream into a heatproof bowl or jug. Heat, uncovered, stirring every minute, for 2 minutes on MEDIUM–HIGH/ *650 watts/70% or until the chocolate cream mixture is smooth.*

Combine the gelatine and water in a small heatproof bowl. Heat, uncovered, for 20–30 seconds on HIGH/800 watts/ *100%, until the gelatine has dissolved.*

150 g white chocolate melts

¼ cup pouring or thickened cream

2 cups mango purée (2 large mangoes, peeled and cored)

¾ cup caster sugar

¼ cup orange juice

2 teaspoons gelatine

3 teaspoons cold water

2 cups country-style natural yoghurt

sliced mango, to serve (optional)

1   Place the white melts and cream in a small saucepan and cook over a low heat, stirring constantly until the chocolate has melted and the mixture is smooth. (Alternatively, see the first microwave tip.) Allow the chocolate cream mixture to cool.

2   Combine the mango purée, sugar and orange juice in a large bowl.

3   Combine the gelatine and water in a small saucepan and cook over a medium heat, stirring constantly, until the gelatine has dissolved. (Alternatively, see the second microwave tip.) Allow the gelatine mixture to cool slightly, then stir into the chocolate cream mixture.

4   Combine the chocolate cream mixture with the yoghurt and the mango mixture and stir well. Pour the yoghurt mixture into a freezerproof container, cover and place in the freezer for 4–6 hours. Transfer the yoghurt mixture to a food processor and process until smooth. Refreeze the yoghurt mixture for a further 4–6 hours, or until firm.

5   Serve the frozen yoghurt with sliced mango, if desired.

Mark's Almond Crescents

One night, after giving a friend some cooking advice, he promised to give me this recipe. It's so good, I had to include it in this book.

MAKES:
approximately 30
PREPARATION TIME:
30 minutes
COOKING TIME:
15 minutes

These biscuits are delicious made with hazelnuts or macadamia nuts. Try roasting the nuts first, in either the oven or the microwave.

200 g unblanched almonds
250 g butter
¹/₃ cup caster sugar

2½ cups plain flour, sifted
1 tablespoon cocoa
100 g dark chocolate melts, melted

1 Preheat the oven to 180°C (350°F). Grease 2 baking trays and line them with non-stick baking paper.

2 Place the almonds in a food processor and pulse until they are finely ground.

3 Place the butter and sugar in a large bowl and cream them until light and fluffy. Add the flour and cocoa and half the almonds, and mix to form a firm dough.

4 Roll the dough into 7-cm lengths, using 1 tablespoon of the mixture for each length. Carefully roll the lengths of dough in the remaining almonds, shape into crescents and place onto the prepared trays.

5 Place the trays in the oven and bake for about 12 minutes, or until the biscuits are light golden in colour. Leave the biscuits to cool on the trays. When they are cold, pipe or drizzle over the dark melts and allow to set before serving.

Choc-swirl Pecan Cake

SERVES: *8–10*

PREPARATION TIME: *25 minutes*

COOKING TIME: *1 hour 10 minutes*

If you do not have a kugelhopf tin you may use a 23-cm round or square cake tin. You may need to cover the cake loosely with a sheet of aluminium foil for the last 20 minutes to prevent it from over-browning.

Place the dark melts and cream in a small heatproof bowl. Heat, uncovered, for 2 minutes on MEDIUM–HIGH/ *650 watts/70%, stirring until the mixture is well combined.*

125 g dark chocolate melts

2 tablespoons pouring or thickened cream

1¼ cups pecans, finely chopped

250 g butter, softened

250 g cream cheese, softened

1 teaspoon grated lemon rind

1 teaspoon vanilla essence

1½ cups caster sugar

4 eggs

1½ cups self-raising flour, sifted

icing sugar, for dusting

extra cream, to serve (optional)

1   Preheat the oven to 160°C (315°F). Grease a 2-litre kugelhopf tin.

2   Place the dark melts and cream in a small saucepan and cook over low heat, stirring constantly, until the chocolate has melted and the mixture is smooth. (Alternatively, see the microwave tip.) Set aside.

3   Scatter ½ cup of the pecans over the base of the prepared tin, reserving the remainder for the cake.

4   Beat the butter, cream cheese, lemon rind, vanilla essence and sugar until soft and smooth. Beat in the eggs one at a time. Do not be concerned if the mixture curdles.

5   Fold the flour and the remaining ¾ cup of the pecans into the cake mixture. Spoon half of the cake mixture into the prepared tin. Pour the chocolate mixture over the cake batter to form a layer and gently spoon over the remaining cake batter. Swirl the cake mixture with a table knife to marble the chocolate layer.

6   Place the cake in the oven and bake for 1 hour 10 minutes, or until a skewer inserted in the centre of the cake comes out clean. Allow the cake to stand for 10 minutes before unmoulding onto a wire cake rack.

7   Dust the cake with icing sugar and serve it at room temperature, with cream if desired.

Flourless Orange and Almond Cake

The original recipe for this popular cake appeared in Claudia Roden's Middle Eastern Cookbook. *This is my version.*

SERVES: 8

PREPARATION TIME:
15 minutes

COOKING TIME:
2½ hours

3 small oranges
250 g unblanched almonds
1 cup caster sugar
⅓ cup Nestlé White Choc Bits
6 eggs
1 teaspoon baking powder

pure cream and hot Chocolate
Sauce, to serve (see page 65)
(optional)

Expect this cake to sink slightly in the centre, as most flourless cakes do.

Place oranges in a medium heatproof bowl and cover with warm water. Cook, uncovered, for 30 minutes on MEDIUM/500 watts/ 50% or until oranges are tender, topping up the water level if necessary.

1. Wash the oranges well. Place the whole oranges in a medium saucepan and cover with warm water. Bring to the boil on a medium heat, then reduce the heat to low and simmer, covered, for 1½ hours, or until the oranges are tender. Top up the water level if necessary. (Alternatively, see the microwave tip.)

2. Preheat the oven to 150°C (300°F). Grease a deep 20-cm springform tin and line with non-stick baking paper.

3. Place the almonds and sugar in the bowl of a food processor and process to a medium texture. Add the white Choc Bits and pulse for a further 30 seconds or until the white Choc Bits are the same texture as the almonds. Transfer the mixture to a large bowl.

4. Drain the oranges and cut them into quarters. Place the oranges (skin, pips and all) in the bowl of a food processor and process until smooth. With the motor running, add the eggs one at a time down the feeding tube, mixing well after each addition. Add the baking powder and blend well.

5. Fold the orange mixture into the almond mixture until just combined. Pour the mixture into the prepared tin and place in the oven. Bake for 1 hour, or until a skewer inserted in the centre of the cake comes out clean. Allow the cake to stand in the tin for 15 minutes before turning it out.

6. Serve at room temperature with pure cream and hot Chocolate Sauce, if desired.

Poppy Seed Muffins

MAKES: *12*

PREPARATION TIME:
10 minutes

COOKING TIME:
25 minutes

125 g butter

1 teaspoon each lemon, lime and
    orange rind

²/₃ cup caster sugar

2 eggs

2 cups self-raising flour, sifted

¹/₃ cup milk

2 tablespoons poppy seeds

1 cup Nestlé Milk Choc Bits

whipped cream, to serve (optional)

*To avoid tough,
heavy muffins never
over mix the batter
when folding in the
dry ingredients.*

1   Grease 2 × 6 (¹/₃-cup capacity) muffin tins. Preheat the oven to 200°C
(390°F).

2   Cream the butter, lemon rind, lime rind, orange rind and sugar until light and
fluffy. Add the eggs one at a time, mixing well after each addition.

3   Gently fold in the flour, milk, poppy seeds and milk Choc Bits.

4   Spoon the batter into the prepared tins and place in the oven. Bake for
20–25 minutes.

5   Serve hot with whipped cream, if desired.

Banana Date Health Loaf

SERVES: 8

PREPARATION TIME:
10 minutes

COOKING TIME:
1 hour 25 minutes

2 medium bananas will give you approximately 1 cup of mashed banana.

To soften butter or cream cheese, cut into even-sized cubes and heat in 1-minute bursts on MEDIUM–LOW/350 watts/30% until soft.

CAKE

2¼ cups wholemeal self-raising
   flour
1 cup dates, finely chopped
½ cup raw sugar
½ cup pecans, chopped
100 g butter, melted
1 cup milk

grated rind of 1 orange
2 eggs, beaten
1 cup mashed banana

LIGHT CHOCOLATE SPREAD

125 g light cream cheese, softened
75 g milk chocolate melts, melted

1. Preheat the oven to 180°C (350°F). Grease a 24 × 13.5-cm loaf tin and line it with non-stick baking paper.

2. *CAKE* Sift the flour into a large bowl, adding back the husks from the sieve. Add the dates, sugar and pecans, mixing to combine.

3. Combine the butter, milk, orange rind, eggs and banana, then add to the dry ingredients and gently mix to combine.

4. Pour the mixture into the prepared loaf tin. Place in the oven and bake for 1 hour 25 minutes, or until golden or cooked (when a skewer inserted in the centre of the cake comes out clean). Allow the cake to cool for 15 minutes in the tin before turning it out.

5. *LIGHT CHOCOLATE SPREAD* Beat the cream cheese in a medium bowl until smooth. Stir in the milk melts until well combined.

6. Serve slices of the loaf covered with the chocolate spread.

Shortbread Twists

MAKES: *16*
PREPARATION TIME:
25 minutes and
chilling time
COOKING TIME:
15–20 minutes
CHILLING TIME:
30 minutes

Rice flour is also
known as ground
rice. It is available
from most
supermarkets.

1 cup plain flour
1 cup rice flour
²/₃ cup icing sugar
175 g butter, chilled and cubed

1 egg
2 tablespoons milk
2 tablespoons cocoa
icing sugar, for dusting

1   Preheat the oven to 160°C (315°F). Line 2 baking trays with non-stick baking paper.

2   Combine the flours and icing sugar in the bowl of a food processor, then pulse for 30 seconds to combine. Add the butter and process until the mixture resembles fine breadcrumbs. Add the egg and milk and process until the mixture comes together.

3   Transfer half the biscuit mixture to a floured surface and knead lightly until the dough is smooth. Wrap the dough in non-stick baking paper and chill for 15 minutes. Add the cocoa to the remaining half of the biscuit mixture and process until well combined. Transfer the chocolate dough to a floured surface, knead lightly until smooth, then wrap in non-stick baking paper and chill for 15 minutes or until firm enough to shape.

4   Using approximately 3 teaspoons of the plain mixture at a time, shape thin 12-cm-long rolls. Repeat using the chocolate mixture. Twist one plain and one chocolate roll together. Place the twists onto the prepared trays and bake in the oven for 15–20 minutes. Allow the twists to cool for 5 minutes on the tray before transferring them to a wire rack.

5   Dust lightly with icing sugar and serve.

Chocolate Caramel Ice-cream

*When you try this recipe, you'll find it hard to believe that it happened by accident –
it's so delicious. I hope you enjoy it.*

SERVES: 6–8
PREPARATION TIME:
10 minutes
COOKING TIME:
10 minutes
FREEZING TIME:
overnight

*Place the sweetened
condensed milk,
butter and golden
syrup in a large
heatproof bowl.
Heat, uncovered,
stirring every
minute, for
4–5 minutes on
HIGH/800 watts/
100%, or until the
mixture turns to
caramel. Remove the
caramel from the
microwave and add
the dark melts,
stirring until the
chocolate has
melted.*

400 g sweetened condensed milk
50 g butter
1 tablespoon golden syrup

100 g dark chocolate melts
2 litres good-quality vanilla
  ice-cream

1 Combine the sweetened condensed milk, butter and golden syrup in a
   medium saucepan and cook over a medium–low heat, stirring constantly,
   until the mixture turns to caramel, about 6–8 minutes. (Alternatively, see the
   microwave tip.) Remove the caramel from the heat and transfer it to a
   heatproof bowl.

2 Add the dark melts to the caramel and stir until the chocolate has melted.
   Allow the chocolate and caramel mixture to cool.

3 Remove the ice-cream from the freezer and allow it to soften at room
   temperature for about 30 minutes. Transfer the ice-cream to a large mixing
   bowl, then swirl through the cooled chocolate caramel. Do not over mix.
   Place the chocolate caramel ice-cream mixture back into the ice-cream
   container and freeze overnight.

Brazil and Coconut Fruit Cake

This cake is great at Christmas time; however, it is so good it should be enjoyed all year round.

SERVES: 8–10

PREPARATION TIME: *approximately 1 hour (including making toffee nuts) plus 2–3 days' marinating time*

COOKING TIME: *1½ hours (20 minutes in the microwave)*

If you do not have time to soak the fruit in the rum, follow step 3 in the microwave instructions on page 112. The result will be the same.

CAKE

200 g sultanas
100 g raisins
100 g dried apricots, chopped
50 g dried apple, chopped
100 g dried figs, chopped
100 g dates, chopped
75 g glacé fruit, chopped (figs, apricots, pineapple or cherries)
¼ cup Malibu White Rum
½ cup shredded coconut
100 g brazil nuts, roughly chopped
150 g butter
¼ cup brown sugar

2 eggs
½ cup Nestlé Dark Choc Bits
½ cup Nestlé White Choc Bits
¼ cup plum jam
½ cup plain flour, sifted
½ teaspoon baking powder
½ teaspoon nutmeg
½ teaspoon cinnamon

TOFFEE BRAZIL NUTS

1 cup sugar
½ cup water
250 g brazil nuts

1   *CAKE*   Combine all the fruit with the rum in a large bowl and allow to marinate for 2–3 days, stirring occasionally. (Alternatively, see the microwave tip.)

2   Preheat the oven to 130°C (265°F). Grease a 23-cm straight-sided ring tin and line with non-stick baking paper.

3   Place the coconut and brazil nuts on a baking tray. Place the tray in the oven and roast for 5–10 minutes, or until the coconut is golden.

4   Cream the butter and brown sugar until thick. Add the eggs one at a time, beating well after each addition. Stir the dark Choc Bits, white Choc Bits and plum jam into the batter.

5   Fold in the sifted dry ingredients, fruit and toasted coconut and brazil nuts. Spread the mixture into the prepared tin. Place the cake in the oven and bake for 1–1½ hours, or until a skewer inserted in the centre of the cake comes out clean. Allow the cake to cool before turning out.

6   *TOFFEE BRAZIL NUTS*   Place the sugar and water in a small saucepan and cook over a medium heat, stirring constantly until the sugar has dissolved. Cease stirring and allow the syrup to simmer until light golden in colour, approximately 30 minutes. Remove the toffee from the heat and drop in the brazil nuts one at a time, coating them in the toffee. Place the nuts on a sheet of non-stick baking paper to set.

7   To serve, decorate the cake with the nuts. ➤

- Grease a 23-cm straight-sided heatproof ring container and line with non-stick baking paper.
- Place the coconut and brazil nuts in an oven bag. Place in the microwave and cook for 3–4 minutes on HIGH/800 watts/100%, removing and shaking the bag every minute.
- Combine all the fruit with the rum in a large heatproof bowl, cover, and heat in the microwave for 8–10 minutes on LOW/90 watts/10%. Allow the fruit to cool slightly.
- Cream the butter and brown sugar until thick. Add the eggs one at a time, beating well after each addition. Stir the dark Choc Bits, white Choc Bits and plum jam into the batter.
- Fold in the sifted dry ingredients, fruit and toasted coconut and brazil nuts. Spread the mixture into the prepared container. Place the cake on a microwave-safe rack and cook, uncovered, for 17–20 minutes on MEDIUM/500 watts/50%. Allow the cake to cool before turning out.
- To make the Toffee Brazil Nuts, place the sugar and water in a heatproof and microwave-safe jug. Heat, uncovered, for 2 minutes on HIGH/800 watts/100%. Stir well to ensure that the sugar has dissolved. Place back in the microwave and cook for 17–20 minutes, uncovered, without stirring, until the syrup turns a light golden colour. Remove the toffee from the heat and drop in the brazil nuts one at a time, coating them in the toffee. Place the nuts on a sheet of non-stick baking paper to set.

Easy Entertaining

How many times have you seen recipes under the title of 'Easy Entertaining', and tried them with devastating results? I am confident that this will not happen with the recipes that follow in this chapter. I have one cooking rule I will never break that I would like to share with you: never cook a recipe for the first time when you are entertaining. Murphy's Law (if something can possibly go wrong, it will) is testimony to that. When you are finally ready to serve these recipes to your guests, I guarantee they will be left wanting just a little bit more!

White Cherry Creme Brulée

I know many people who have tried unsuccessfully to make creme brulée. The white chocolate in this recipe helps to set the brulée and keep it firm while grilling.

SERVES: 6–8
PREPARATION TIME:
*40 minutes plus
chilling time*
COOKING TIME:
20–30 minutes
CHILLING TIME:
*overnight plus
40 minutes*

*Many professional
kitchens use a blow
torch to caramelise
the sugar on a
brulée. Surprisingly,
they are easy to use
and affordable at
most hardware
stores – for the
brulée enthusiasts!*

*Heat the cream and
vanilla bean in a
microwave-safe jug,
uncovered, for 2–3
minutes on HIGH/
800 watts/100%.*

2 cups pure cream
1 vanilla bean
6 egg yolks
½ cup caster sugar
200 g white chocolate melts

375 g cherries, pitted and halved
extra ¼ cup caster sugar

extra cherries, to serve (optional)

1. Place the cream in a heavy-based saucepan. Split the vanilla bean in half lengthwise and scrape the black seeds into the cream, adding the pod also. Bring the vanilla cream to the boil. (Alternatively, see the microwave tip.) Remove the cream from the heat immediately.

2. Meanwhile, whisk the egg yolks with the sugar in a medium mixing bowl until well blended. Pour the hot vanilla cream into the egg mixture, whisking constantly. Discard the vanilla pod. Return the mixture to the saucepan and cook over a low heat, stirring constantly, until the mixture coats the back of a metal spoon, 20–30 minutes.

3. Remove the custard from the heat and strain into a bowl. Add the white melts, and whisk until the chocolate has melted and the custard is smooth.

4. Place the cherries over the base of a 2-litre heatproof dish or 6 individual heatproof serving bowls. Pour the custard and chocolate mixture over the cherries, all the way to the top. Cover the custard/s and refrigerate overnight.

5. 1 hour before serving, sprinkle the top of the custard/s with caster sugar, then brown the sugar under a very hot grill. When all the sugar has melted and caramelised, sprinkle on a second layer of sugar and repeat the grilling process. Allow the brulée/s to chill for 40 minutes, then serve with extra cherries, if desired.

Apricot and Pistachio Truffles

MAKES:
approximately 30
PREPARATION TIME:
40 minutes
COOKING TIME:
5 minutes
CHILLING TIME:
3 hours

200 g Marie biscuits, crushed
50 g pistachio nuts, ground
1 cup icing sugar
200 g dried apricots, finely
  chopped
50 g butter
100 g milk chocolate melts
2 tablespoons maple syrup

4 tablespoons strong black coffee
2 tablespoons Marsala
1 cup Rice Bubbles or chopped
  nuts
200 g white or milk chocolate
  melts
50 g copha

*Place the butter,
100 g milk melts,
maple syrup, coffee
and Marsala in a
small heatproof
bowl. Heat,
uncovered, for
2–3 minutes on
MEDIUM–HIGH/650
watts/70%, stirring
until well combined.*

*Place the copha in a
small heatproof bowl.
Heat, uncovered, for
3–4 minutes on
MEDIUM–HIGH/650
watts/70%, or until
the copha has
melted. Remove the
copha from the
microwave and add
the white or milk
melts. The heat
from the copha will
melt the chocolate.
Stir well to combine.*

1   Combine the biscuit crumbs, nuts, icing sugar and apricots in a large bowl; mix well.

2   Place the butter, 100 g milk melts, maple syrup, coffee and Marsala in a small saucepan and cook over a medium heat, stirring constantly, until the chocolate and butter have melted and the mixture is smooth. (Alternatively, see the first microwave tip.) Cool the mixture slightly. Add the chocolate mixture to the biscuit mixture and mix well.

3   Roll the mixture into walnut-sized balls using moist hands. Roll the balls in the Rice Bubbles or nuts and coat evenly. Place the truffles on a tray lined with non-stick baking paper and refrigerate until firm.

4   Place the white or milk melts and copha in a small saucepan, and cook over a low heat, stirring constantly, until the chocolate has melted. (Alternatively, see the second microwave tip.) Remove the mixture from the heat. Using 2 forks, carefully coat the truffles in the chocolate and allow them to set on the baking tray. Refrigerate the truffles until ready to serve.

5   Serve truffles at room temperature.

Temporary Insanity

This decadent, delicious dessert was developed for Karen at Lintas Sprint. Whenever we have chocolate-tasting panels, she (and many others) temporarily go insane.

SERVES: 6–8

PREPARATION TIME:
30 minutes

COOKING TIME:
30 minutes

CHILLING TIME:
3–4 hours

When chilling pastry, wrap it in non-stick baking paper. Plastic will cause the pastry to sweat.

Any liqueur may be used: Grand Marnier, Bailey's or Tia Maria all work well.

Place the chocolate and creams in a heatproof bowl. Heat, uncovered, stirring every minute, for 4–5 minutes on MEDIUM/500 watts/ 50% or until smooth.

PASTRY

1½ cups plain flour
⅓ cup icing sugar
125 g butter, chilled and cubed
1 egg yolk
2 teaspoons cold water

CHOCOLATE FILLING

300 g cooking chocolate
300 ml pure cream
100 ml pouring cream
2 tablespoons chocolate liqueur
2 eggs, separated
pinch of cream of tartar

cocoa, for dusting
whipped cream, to serve

1 *PASTRY* Combine the flour and icing sugar in the bowl of a food processor. Pulse the dry ingredients for 30 seconds to combine. Add the butter and process until the mixture resembles fine breadcrumbs. Add the egg yolk and water and process the mixture until the dough comes together. Transfer the dough to a lightly floured surface. Knead the dough lightly and wrap it in non-stick baking paper. Chill for 20 minutes.

2 Preheat the oven to 180°C (350°F). Lightly grease a 25-cm flan tin.

3 Roll out the pastry to form a 28 × 30-cm rectangle. Line the prepared flan tin with the pastry. Bake blind (see page ix for tip) for 15 minutes. Remove the aluminium foil and beans and set aside. Cook the pastry case for a further 12–15 minutes, or until it is golden. Allow the pastry to cool completely.

4 *CHOCOLATE FILLING* Place the chocolate, pure cream and pouring cream into a medium saucepan. Cook over a low heat, stirring constantly, until the chocolate has melted and the mixture is smooth. (Alternatively, see the microwave tip.) Remove the chocolate mixture from the heat and transfer to a large bowl. Add the liqueur and egg yolks, mixing well. Allow the chocolate mixture to cool. Beat the egg whites with the cream of tartar until soft peaks form, then fold into the chocolate mixture.

5 Carefully pour the Chocolate Filling into the pastry case, then refrigerate the tart for 3–4 hours or until set.

6 Dust with cocoa just before serving and serve with whipped cream.

Macadamia Pie

SERVES: 8

PREPARATION TIME:
*25 minutes plus
chilling time*

COOKING TIME:
*approximately
1 hour*

CHILLING TIME:
45 minutes

*Corn syrup is a
thick, sweet syrup
available in light
and dark from most
supermarkets and
delicatessens.*

*Frangelico is a
hazelnut liqueur
which may be
substituted with any
liqueur or strong
black coffee.*

PASTRY
1½ cups plain flour
125 g butter, chilled and cubed
1 egg yolk
3 teaspoons cold water
200 g macadamia nuts, roughly
    chopped

FILLING
⅔ cup brown sugar
2 tablespoons plain flour
3 eggs

1 cup light corn syrup
1 teaspoon vanilla essence
2 tablespoons Frangelico liqueur
30 g butter, melted
100 g cooking chocolate, melted

pure cream or frozen yoghurt, to
    serve

1   PASTRY   Place the flour and butter into the bowl of a food processor. Process until the mixture resembles fine breadcrumbs. Add the egg yolk and water, then process until the mixture comes together in a ball. Transfer the dough to a floured surface; knead gently for 1–2 minutes. Pat the dough into a 15-cm round shape, wrap in non-stick baking paper and chill in the refrigerator for 30 minutes.

2   Preheat the oven to 180°C (350°F). Grease a 23 cm deep pie plate.

3   Roll out the pastry between sheets of lightly floured non-stick baking paper to a 26-cm round. Place the pastry into the prepared pie plate, making sure the base and sides are covered. Trim the edges and decorate the edge of the pie with pastry shapes if desired. Chill in the refrigerator for 15 minutes.

4   Sprinkle the macadamia nuts over the chilled pastry.

5   FILLING   Meanwhile, combine the sugar, flour, eggs, corn syrup, vanilla essence and Frangelico, mixing well. Whisk in the butter and chocolate, then pour the mixture into the pastry case. Place in the oven and bake for about 1 hour, or until the centre is cooked (when a skewer inserted into the centre of the pie comes out clean). If necessary, loosely cover the pie with a sheet of aluminium foil 20 minutes before the end of cooking to prevent the top over-browning.

6   Serve the pie warm with pure cream or frozen yoghurt.

Citrus Crumble Cake

The combination of sweet and sour with crisp and soft makes this cake a real favourite with all who consume it.

SERVES: *8–10*

PREPARATION TIME:
30 minutes and chilling time

COOKING TIME:
30 minutes

CHILLING TIME:
2 hours

Place the eggs, sugar, lemon and lime juice, lime rind and butter in a heatproof bowl. Cook, uncovered, whisking every minute, for 4–6 minutes on MEDIUM/*500 watts/ 50%, or until thick.*

FILLING

3 eggs
$^1/_3$ cup caster sugar
$^1/_4$ cup lemon juice
$^1/_4$ cup lime juice
grated rind of 1 lime
60 g butter, softened
100 g white chocolate melts, melted

PASTRY

$1^1/_2$ cups self-raising flour
$^1/_3$ cup caster sugar
100 g butter, chilled and cubed
2 eggs
1 tablespoon cocoa

1 FILLING   Place the eggs, sugar, lemon and lime juice, lime rind and butter into a heatproof bowl. Place the bowl over a pan of simmering water, making sure that the base does not sit in the water. Whisk the mixture constantly using an electric handmixer on low speed for 6–8 minutes, or until mixture thickens. (Alternatively, see the microwave tip.) Remove the mixture from the heat and stir in the white melts, mixing well to ensure the mixture is smooth. Allow the mixture to cool.

2 Preheat the oven to 180°C (350°F). Grease a 20-cm springform cake tin.

3 PASTRY   Place the flour and sugar in the bowl of a food processor. Pulse for 30 seconds to combine. Add the butter and process until the mixture resembles fine breadcrumbs. Add the eggs and process until the mixture comes together. Remove one-third of the dough, wrap it in non-stick baking paper and freeze until it is firm, approximately 2 hours. Meanwhile, add the cocoa to the remaining dough in the processor and process to combine.

4 Press the chocolate pastry into the base of the prepared tin and cook for 10 minutes. Remove the chocolate pastry from the oven and carefully pour in the citrus filling. Place the tin onto a baking tray. Bake for a further 15 minutes. Remove the cake from the oven and allow to cool. Take the reserved pastry from the freezer and coarsely grate it over the cake. Place the cake under a preheated grill and grill the top until it is light golden in colour. Cool the cake in the tin. Serve.

Ricotta and Pinenut Crumble Cake

I shared this dessert with a friend at a fabulous cafe in Surry Hills, Sydney, and I promised I would come up with a similar recipe. Here it is!

SERVES: *8–10*
PREPARATION TIME:
25 minutes plus chilling time
COOKING TIME:
50 minutes
CHILLING TIME:
overnight plus 45 minutes

Mascarpone is Italian cream cheese. It is smooth and delicious, and is available at delicatessens and most supermarkets. You can use soft cream cheese as a substitute.

PASTRY

¾ **cup self-raising flour**
½ **cup plain flour**
¼ **cup ground almonds**
¼ **cup caster sugar**
100 g **softened butter**
1 **egg**
grated rind of 1 lemon

FILLING

500 g **fresh ricotta cheese**
½ **cup caster sugar**
1 teaspoon **vanilla essence**
200 g **mascarpone**
1 tablespoon **plain flour**
2 tablespoons **Tia Maria**
½ **cup toasted pinenuts**
⅔ **cup Nestlé Dark Choc Bits, roughly chopped**

pure cream, to serve (optional)

1   *PASTRY*   Place all the pastry ingredients in the bowl of a food processor and process until the pastry comes together. Transfer the dough to a lightly floured surface and knead gently for 1–2 minutes. Remove one-third of the pastry, then wrap it in non-stick baking paper and freeze. Pat out the remaining pastry to a rectangular shape, wrap in non-stick baking paper and chill in the refrigerator for 30 minutes.

2   Preheat the oven to 180°C (350°F). Grease a 28 × 18-cm lamington tin.

3   Remove the larger piece of pastry from the refrigerator. Roll out the pastry so it will fit the base and sides of the prepared tin. Don't be concerned if it breaks a little; mould it back together in the tin. Chill in the refrigerator for 15 minutes.

4   *FILLING*   Meanwhile, using an electric mixer, beat the ricotta, sugar and vanilla essence until the cheese is smooth and the ingredients have combined. Add the mascarpone, and mix on a low speed until just combined. Fold in the remaining filling ingredients.

5   Spread the ricotta mixture over the chilled pastry in the lamington tin. Coarsely grate the remaining frozen pastry over the filling.

6   Place the cake in the oven and bake for 40–50 minutes, or until the top is golden and the filling is cooked (when a skewer is inserted in the centre of the cake it should come out clean). Allow the cake to cool at room temperature and then refrigerate overnight.

7   Cut the cake into squares and serve at room temperature with pure cream, if desired.

Truffle Cake

This cake looks and tastes decadent and was developed for Katrina at Channel 9, who loves chocolate even more than I.

SERVES: 8

PREPARATION TIME: *40 minutes and cooling time*

COOKING TIME: *55 minutes*

¾ cup milk

3 tablespoons espresso ground coffee

185 g softened butter

¾ cup caster sugar

3 eggs

150 g cooking chocolate, melted

1¼ cups self-raising flour, sifted

½ cup plain flour, sifted

⅓ cup cocoa

300 ml pouring or thickened cream, whipped

Chocolate Ganache (see page 65)

214 g Baci Chocolates

Place the milk in a heatproof bowl or jug. Heat, uncovered, for 1½ minutes on HIGH/ 800 watts/100%.

1 Preheat the oven to 180°C (350°F). Grease a 20-cm springform cake tin and line with non-stick baking paper.

2 Place the milk in a small saucepan and bring to the boil. (Alternatively, see the microwave tip.)

3 Meanwhile, cream the butter and sugar until light and fluffy. Add the eggs one at a time, mixing well after each addition. Don't be concerned if the mixture curdles. Add the chocolate and mix well.

4 Fold in the combined flours and cocoa with the coffee-flavoured milk. Spread the mixture into the prepared tin and place in the oven. Bake for 40–45 minutes, or until a skewer inserted in the centre of the cake comes out clean. Allow the cake to stand for 10 minutes in the tin before turning it out onto a wire rack to cool.

5 When the cake is cold, cut it in half lengthwise with a serrated knife. Place the base cake onto the serving plate and top with the cream. Carefully place the remaining cake on top. Cover the top and side of the cake with two-thirds of the Chocolate Ganache, using the remaining one-third to pipe rosettes around the edges. Decorate the cake with the Baci Chocolates.

Sour Cream Berry Tartlets

I first tasted these heavenly tartlets on a Club Med holiday in Bali.

MAKES: 24
PREPARATION TIME:
10 minutes
COOKING TIME:
25 minutes

These tartlets are best made using fresh fruit. Any berries may be used – blueberries, blackberries, strawberries, etc.

24 frozen sweet shortcrust tartlet cases
100 g cooking chocolate, melted
300 g sour cream
½ cup caster sugar
1 teaspoon vanilla essence
1 tablespoon plain flour
grated rind of 1 lemon
1 tablespoon lemon juice
⅓ cup toasted slivered almonds
300 g fresh or frozen raspberries
extra caster sugar

1   Preheat the oven to 180°C (350°F).

2   Place the tartlet cases, leaving the pastry in the foil cases, onto 2 baking trays. Place the trays in the oven and bake the cases for 8–10 minutes, or until the pastry is light golden in colour. Cool slightly.

3   Brush each tartlet case with the melted chocolate.

4   Combine the sour cream, sugar, vanilla essence, flour, lemon rind and juice. Carefully fold in the almonds and the raspberries until just combined. Spoon the mixture into the chocolate tartlet cases. Sprinkle each tartlet with extra sugar and place back into the oven for 10–15 minutes, or until the custard is firm. Serve warm.

Chewy Pecan Bars

In 1996 I presented many recipes to the fabulous, creative team at Lintas Sprint. These Chewy Pecan Bars were one of the favourites.

MAKES:
approximately 20
PREPARATION TIME:
15 minutes
COOKING TIME:
50 minutes

Place the milk melts and sweetened condensed milk in a large heatproof bowl. Heat, uncovered, stirring every minute, for 3–4 minutes on MEDIUM–HIGH/650 watts/70%, or until well combined.

BASE
1½ cups plain flour
½ cup icing sugar
125 g butter, softened
100 g white chocolate melts, melted

TOPPING
200 g milk chocolate melts
400 g sweetened condensed milk
2 eggs
3 tablespoons plain flour
2 cups pecan nuts

1   Preheat the oven to 180°C (350°F). Grease a 28 × 18-cm lamington tin and line with non-stick baking paper.

2   *BASE*   Using an electric mixer or food processor, mix the plain flour, icing sugar, butter and white melts until well combined. Press the mixture into the base of the prepared tin. Place in the oven and bake for 15 minutes, or until light golden in colour. Cool slightly. Reduce the oven temperature to 160°C (315°F).

3   *TOPPING*   In a small saucepan, combine the milk melts and sweetened condensed milk. Cook over a medium heat, stirring constantly, until the chocolate has melted. (Alternatively, see the microwave tip.) Remove the chocolate and milk from the heat and cool slightly. Stir in the eggs, flour and pecans.

4   Pour the pecan mixture over the base. Bake the slice for a further 30–35 minutes, or until a skewer inserted in the centre of the slice comes out clean. The mixture may be a little soft; however, it will firm on cooling. Refrigerate the slice for 3–4 hours before cutting it into squares.

Frozen Chocolate Tiramisu

This is one of those fabulous entertaining recipes that can be made 1–2 days ahead.

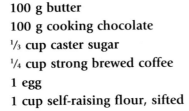

SERVES: 8
PREPARATION TIME:
30 minutes and
freezing time
COOKING TIME:
25 minutes
FREEZING TIME:
overnight

This dessert is better if it is allowed to stand at room temperature for 15–20 minutes (depending on air temperature) before serving.

Combine the butter and chocolate in a large heatproof bowl. Heat, uncovered, for 2–3 minutes on MEDIUM/500 watts/ 50%. Stir the butter and chocolate until well combined.

100 g butter
100 g cooking chocolate
⅓ cup caster sugar
¼ cup strong brewed coffee
1 egg
1 cup self-raising flour, sifted

MASCARPONE FILLING

2 eggs, separated
½ cup caster sugar

250 g mascarpone or soft cream cheese
300 ml thickened cream, whipped
2 teaspoons coffee powder
½ cup Nestlé White Choc Bits, roughly chopped
Marsala

cocoa, for dusting
Chocolate Sauce (see page 65), to serve

1 Preheat the oven to 180°C (350°F). Grease a 20-cm springform cake tin and line it with non-stick baking paper.

2 Combine the butter and chocolate in a small saucepan. Cook over a low heat, stirring constantly, until the mixture is smooth. (Alternatively, see the microwave tip.) Transfer the mixture to a large mixing bowl.

3 Add the sugar, coffee, egg and flour. Pour the mixture into the prepared tin, place in the oven and bake for 25 minutes. Allow the cake to stand in the tin for 10 minutes, then turn it out onto a wire rack to cool.

4 *MASCARPONE FILLING*   Using an electric mixer, beat the egg yolks and sugar until light and creamy. Fold in the mascarpone and half the whipped cream until well combined. Reserve the remaining cream for serving.

5 Add the coffee to the cream mixture. Beat the egg whites until firm and fold through the cream mixture gently with the white Choc Bits.

6 Line the springform tin with plastic wrap. Slice the cooled cake in half lengthwise and place the bottom half back into the springform tin. Drizzle the cake with Marsala. Pour in the filling and top with the remaining cake. Press down well to get rid of any air pockets. Cover the cake with more plastic wrap and place it in the freezer for at least 5 hours (overnight, if possible) or until completely frozen.

7 Remove the cake from the freezer and slide it onto a serving plate, removing the plastic wrap. Before slicing, cover the cake with the reserved whipped cream and dust well with cocoa. Cut the cake into wedges with a hot knife and serve drizzled with hot Chocolate Sauce.

Chunky Chocolate Macadamia Fudge Cookies

These cookies are moist and fudgy and are a regular item in my pantry.

MAKES:
approximately 30
PREPARATION TIME:
10 minutes
COOKING TIME:
12 minutes

Try using pistachio nuts or white Choc Bits to vary this recipe.

These cookies are great warm. Heat, uncovered, for 15–20 seconds on MEDIUM/500 watts/ 50%.

1 egg
1 cup brown sugar
1 teaspoon vanilla essence
½ cup canola oil
½ cup self-raising flour, sifted
1 cup plain flour, sifted

200 g cooking chocolate, chopped
150 g macadamia nuts, roughly chopped
½ cup desiccated coconut

1. Preheat the oven to 180°C (350°F). Grease 2–3 baking trays and line with non-stick baking paper. (5) GAS

2. In a large bowl, whisk together the egg, brown sugar, vanilla essence and oil until well combined.

3. Add the flours, chocolate, nuts and coconut to the egg mixture and stir until well combined.

4. Place tablespoonfuls of the mixture onto the prepared trays, allowing a little room for the cookies to spread.

5. Place the trays in the oven and bake for 12 minutes, or until light golden in colour. Allow the cookies to cool for 10 minutes on the trays before transferring them to a wire rack to cool completely.

Panforte

This nutty cake is an Italian specialty from Siena, which is traditionally served at Christmas time.

MAKES: *1 large or 6 individual cakes*
PREPARATION TIME: *20 minutes*
COOKING TIME: *1 hour 20 minutes*

Fruit medley is a dried fruit mix available at all supermarkets.

Wrap the small Panfortes in cellophane and give as Christmas gifts.

Place the nuts in an oven bag, then twist the bag to secure. Place the bag onto a heatproof plate, then cook the nuts in the microwave, shaking the bag every minute, for 3–4 minutes on HIGH/ 800 watts/100%, or until golden.

80 g hazelnuts, roughly chopped
80 g almonds, roughly chopped
¾ cup plain flour
¼ cup cocoa
1 teaspoon cinnamon
½ teaspoon nutmeg
1 teaspoon mixed spice
125 g fruit medley
50 g mixed peel

50 g dried pineapple, chopped
50 g dried pawpaw, chopped
50 g dried mango, chopped
50 g dried figs, chopped
1 cup caster sugar
⅔ cup honey
200 g cooking chocolate, melted
icing sugar, for dusting

1   Preheat the oven to 180°C (350°F). Grease a 23-cm round cake tin and line with non-stick baking paper.

2   Spread the nuts on a baking tray, place in the oven and roast for 10–15 minutes, or until light golden. (Alternatively, see the microwave tip.) Allow the nuts to cool. Reduce the oven temperature to 150°C (300°F).

3   Sift the flour, cocoa and spices into a large bowl. Add the fruit medley, mixed peel, dried fruits and roasted nuts, and mix until the fruit and nuts are coated with the flour mixture.

4   In a small heavy-based saucepan, cook the sugar and honey over a low heat, stirring constantly, until the sugar has dissolved, 5–7 minutes. Allow the sugar mixture to simmer for 8–10 minutes without stirring. It is ready to remove from the heat when a little mixture dropped into cold water forms a soft ball. Add the sugar mixture quickly to the fruit mixture. Mix in the melted chocolate, working as quickly as possible.

5   Tip the dough out onto a bench top and knead until the mixture comes together. Press into the prepared cake tin. Place in the oven and bake for 50–60 minutes, or until a skewer inserted in the centre of the cake comes out clean. (Alternatively, press the mixture into 6 egg rings that have been greased and placed onto a baking tray lined with non-stick baking paper. Do not over fill the rings as the mixture rises slightly. Bake the individual panfortes for 35–40 minutes, or until cooked when tested with a skewer.)

6   Allow the panfortes to cool before serving, then dust generously with icing sugar.

7   Cut the large panforte into wedges; leave the individual panfortes whole. Serve with cheese and fruit.

Deirdre's Chocolate Mousse

Every year my family used to visit friends who lived on a farm. We loved Deirdre's Chocolate Mousse, and here is the secret recipe.

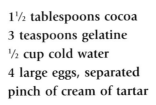

Serves: *6*
PREPARATION TIME:
15 minutes
COOKING TIME:
5 minutes
CHILLING TIME:
3–4 hours

The addition of a pinch of cream of tartar helps to stabilise the eggs while beating.

1½ tablespoons cocoa
3 teaspoons gelatine
½ cup cold water
4 large eggs, separated
pinch of cream of tartar

4 tablespoons caster sugar
1 teaspoon vanilla essence

rolled wafer biscuits and fresh fruit (optional), to serve

1. Combine the cocoa, gelatine and water in a small saucepan, and cook over a medium heat, whisking constantly, until the mixture just comes to the boil and the cocoa has dissolved. Remove the chocolate mixture from the heat and cool to room temperature.

2. Use an electric mixer to beat the egg whites and cream of tartar for 3–5 minutes, or until stiff peaks form. Add the sugar one tablespoonful at a time, mixing well to ensure the sugar has dissolved. Add the vanilla essence and then add the egg yolks one at a time, beating well after each addition.

3. Fold the chocolate mixture into the egg mixture as carefully as possible. Spoon the mousse evenly into a serving bowl or 6 individual glasses, cover and refrigerate for 3–4 hours.

4. Serve the mousse with rolled wafer biscuits and fresh fruit, if desired.

Easy Chocolate Cake

When you are in a real hurry and you want to cook a cake that is quick, easy and impressive, this chocolate cake is the recipe that you are looking for.

SERVES: *8–10*
PREPARATION TIME:
15 minutes
COOKING TIME:
55 minutes

Frozen berries are very handy for emergencies and are ideal when fresh berries are out of season.

150 g butter, softened
1½ cups caster sugar
2 teaspoons vanilla essence
2 eggs
125 g dark chocolate melts or cooking chocolate, melted
2 cups plain flour, sifted
2 teaspoons baking powder
⅔ cup cocoa
1¼ cups milk

TOPPING

250 g strawberries, hulled and halved
125 g blueberries
250 g raspberries
2 tablespoons caster sugar
2 tablespoons Cointreau

whipped or pure cream, to serve

1 Preheat the oven to 180°C (350°F). Grease a 23-cm round cake tin and line with non-stick baking paper.

2 Use an electric handmixer to beat the butter, sugar and vanilla essence until light and fluffy. Add the eggs, one at a time, mixing well after each addition. Add the chocolate, then mix the batter until just combined.

3 Fold in the combined flour, baking powder and cocoa alternately with the milk. Spread the mixture into the prepared tin. Place the cake mixture in the oven and bake for about 50 minutes, or until a skewer inserted in the centre of the cake comes out clean. Allow the cake to cool slightly in the tin before turning it out onto a wire rack to cool completely.

4 *TOPPING*   10 minutes before serving, combine the strawberries, blueberries and raspberries in a large bowl. Sprinkle over the sugar and Cointreau, and mix gently with a rubber spatula, being careful not to bruise the berries. Carefully spoon the berry mixture on top of the cake and serve with cream.

Mocha Ice-cream Sandwich

SERVES: *8*
PREPARATION TIME:
*30 minutes and
freezing time*
COOKING TIME:
15 minutes
FREEZING TIME:
*approximately
10 hours*

125 g cooking chocolate
125 g butter
1 egg
½ cup caster sugar
1½ tablespoons Kahlua or strong
   black coffee
1 teaspoon vanilla essence
¾ cup plain flour
2 tablespoons cocoa

½ teaspoon baking powder
¼ teaspoon cinnamon
1½ litres coffee ice-cream

chocolate curls (see page 5) and
   orange segments, to serve
   (optional)
hot Chocolate Sauce (see page 65)
   (optional), to serve

*Cut the Mocha Ice-
cream Sandwich
with a warm knife.*

*Place the chocolate
and butter in a
large heatproof
bowl. Heat,
uncovered, stirring
every minute, for
3–4 minutes on
MEDIUM/500 watts/
50%.*

1 Preheat the oven to 160°C (315°F). Grease 2 × 28 × 18-cm lamington tins and line them with non-stick baking paper.

2 Melt the chocolate and butter in a small saucepan over a low heat, stirring constantly, until the mixture is smooth. (Alternatively, see the microwave tip.)

3 Beat the egg and sugar until the mixture is thick and creamy. Fold in the chocolate mixture, Kahlua and vanilla essence.

4 Sift together the flour, cocoa, baking powder and cinnamon, then fold the dry ingredients into the chocolate mixture. Divide the batter evenly into the prepared tins. Bake in the oven for 12–15 minutes, or until a skewer inserted in the centre of each cake comes out clean. Cool the cakes in the tins before removing them. Wrap the cakes in aluminium foil and freeze them in their tins for 2–3 hours, or until firm enough to handle.

5 Remove the chocolate cakes from the tins. Peel away the aluminium foil. Line one lamington tin with aluminium foil, then place one cake back into the tin. Top the 'sandwich' base with softened coffee ice-cream and place the second 'sandwich' on top. Cover the sandwich with aluminium foil, place in the freezer and freeze overnight.

6 Decorate with chocolate curls and serve with orange segments and hot Chocolate Sauce if desired.

Profiteroles with Apricot Purée, Custard and Hot Chocolate Sauce

Profiteroles have always been a specialty of mine and consequently are my trademark at many parties. I'm sure they will soon become a specialty of yours.

MAKES: *16 profiteroles*

PREPARATION TIME: *45 minutes*

COOKING TIME: *1 hour 10 minutes*

Place the apricot purée ingredients into a medium heatproof bowl. Cook uncovered for 6–8 minutes on MEDIUM/*500 watts/ 50% or until the apricots have absorbed the liquid and become tender.*

PROFITEROLES
1 cup water
125 g butter
1 cup plain flour
3–4 eggs

CUSTARD
4 egg yolks
²/₃ cup caster sugar
1 teaspoon vanilla essence
6 teaspoons cornflour
2 tablespoons plain flour
600 ml milk

APRICOT PURÉE
125 g dried apricots
½ cup orange juice
grated rind of 1 orange

Chocolate Sauce (see page 65), to serve

1 Preheat the oven to 200°C (390°F). Lightly grease two baking trays.

2 *PROFITEROLES* Place the water and butter into a medium saucepan over a low heat. Allow the butter to melt slowly, stirring occasionally. Once the butter has melted, increase the heat to high and bring the butter to a rapid boil, then remove the pan from the heat and quickly stir in the sifted flour. Mix well, ensuring that the mixture comes together in a ball and that the flour has been cooked.

3 Transfer the mixture to an electric mixer. Add the eggs one at a time, mixing well after each addition. Before adding the last egg, check the consistency: the mixture should be thick and glossy. If the mixture is not quite right, lightly beat the remaining egg and add a little at a time until the right consistency is reached.

4 For each profiterole spoon or pipe tablespoonfuls of mixture onto the prepared trays. Bake for 35–40 minutes or until the puffs are well risen and have dried out. Turn off the oven and leave the pastries to cool in the oven with the door ajar.

5 *CUSTARD* Whisk together the egg yolks, sugar and vanilla essence until light and creamy. Add the cornflour and plain flour and mix well. Pour in the milk and whisk until well combined. Transfer the mixture to a medium saucepan over a medium–low heat and stir constantly until the custard boils and thickens, about 20 minutes. Remove from the heat and pour into a heatproof bowl. Place a piece of plastic wrap directly onto the surface of the custard and allow to cool. Refrigerate for at least 3–4 hours before serving. ➤

6   *APRICOT PURÉE*   Place all the ingredients into a small saucepan over a
     medium heat. Stir occasionally until the apricots absorb all the juice and
     become soft and tender. (Alternatively, see the microwave tip.) Remove from
     the heat and purée in a blender, then leave to cool.

7   Cut the profiteroles in half and place a spoonful of apricot purée into the
     base of each half. Top with the custard, then replace the other profiterole half.
     Serve the filled profiteroles with the hot Chocolate Sauce.

Index

Page numbers in italics refer to recipe photographs.